PUBLIC-PRIVATE PARTNERSHIPS

PUBLIC-PRIVATE PARTNERSHIPS

LESLIE R. KELLERMAN
EDITOR

Nova Science Publishers, Inc.
New York

LIBRARY OF CONGRESS CATALOGING-IN-PUBLICATION DATA

ISBN: 978-1-60692-358-0

Available upon request.

Published by Nova Science Publishers, Inc. ✦ New York

CONTENTS

PREFACE

Chapter 1 - Growing demands on the transportation system and constraints on public resources have led to calls for more private sector involvement in the provision of highway and transit infrastructure through what are known as "public-private partnerships" (PPPs). A PPP, broadly defined, is any arrangement whereby the private sector assumes more responsibility than is traditional for infrastructure planning, financing, design, construction, operation, and maintenance. This new book describes the wide variety of public-private partnerships in highways and transit, but focuses on the two types of highway PPPs that are generating the most debate: the leasing by the public sector to the private sector of existing infrastructure; and the building, leasing, and owning of new infrastructure by private entities. PPP proponents argue that, in addition to being the best hope for injecting additional resources into the surface freight and passenger transportation systems for upkeep and expansion, private sector involvement potentially reduces costs, project delivery time, and public sector risk, and may also improve project selection and project quality. Detractors, on the other hand, argue that the potential for PPPs is limited, and that, unless carefully regulated, PPPs will disrupt the operation of the surface transportation network, increase driving and other costs for the traveling public, and subvert the public planning process. Some of the specific issues raised in highway operation and costs include the effects of PPPs on trucking, low-income households, and traffic diversion. Issues raised in transportation planning include non-compete provisions in PPP agreements, unsolicited proposals, lease duration, and foreign control of transportation assets. On the question of new resources, the evidence suggests that there is significant private funding available for investment in surface transportation infrastructure, but that it is unlikely to amount to more than 10% of the ongoing needs of highways over the next 20 years or so, if that, and probably a much smaller share of transit needs. With competing demands for public funds, there is also a concern that private funding will substitute for public resources with no net gain in transportation infrastructure. The effect of PPPs on the planning and operation of the transportation system is a more open question because of the numerous forms they can take, and because they are dependent on the detailed agreements negotiated between the public and private partners. For this reason, some have suggested that the federal government needs to more systematically identify and evaluate the public interest, particularly the national public interest, in projects that employ a PPP. Three broad policy options Congress might consider in how to deal with PPPs in federal transportation programs and regulations are discussed in this book. The first option is to continue with the current policy of incremental changes and experimentation in program incentives and regulation. Second is to actively encourage PPPs with program incentives, but with relatively tight regulatory controls. Third is to aggressively encourage the use of PPPs through program incentives and limited, if any, regulation.

Chapter 2 - The private sector has traditionally been involved as contractors in the design and construction of highways. In recent years, the private sector has become increasingly involved in assuming other responsibilities including planning, designing, and financing. The private sector has also entered into a wide variety of highway public-private partnership arrangements with public agencies. According to FHWA, the term "public-private-partnership" is used for any scenario under which the private sector assumes a greater role in the planning, financing, design, construction, operation, and maintenance of a transportation facility compared to traditional procurement methods.[5] Under some of these alternative arrangements, the private sector is increasingly being looked at to not only construct facilities but also to finance, maintain, and operate such infrastructure under long-term leaseholds—up to 99 years in some cases. In some cases, this involves financing and constructing a new facility and then operating and maintaining it over a specified period of time, while in other cases it involves operating and maintaining an existing toll road for a period of time in exchange for an up-front payment provided to the public sector. Proponents of these forms of highway public-private partnerships contend that they offer the potential advantages of obtaining critical new or expanded infrastructure sooner than if provided solely by the public sector, at a potentially lower cost given the efficiencies and innovation of market-driven private companies, and the use of private rather than public funds. In addition, risks of major infrastructure projects, such as risks associated with constructing highways and risks of generating sufficient traffic and revenue for financial viability, can be shifted from the public to the private sector. Since these arrangements are often used in relation to toll roads, the private sector return is achieved through the collection of future toll revenue. However, highway public-private partnership arrangements are not "risk free," and concerns have been raised about how well the public interest has been evaluated and protected. Concerns have also been raised about the potential loss of public control over critical assets for up to 99 years.

Chapter 3 provides testimony regarding Highway Public-Private Partnerships, Securing Potential Benefits and Protecting the Public Interest Could Result from More Rigorous up-Front Analysis.

In: Public-Private Partnerships   ISBN: 978-1-60692-358-0
Editor: Leslie R. Kellerman, pp. 1-38   © 2009 Nova Science Publishers, Inc.

Chapter 1

PUBLIC-PRIVATE PARTNERSHIPS IN HIGHWAY AND TRANSIT INFRASTRUCTURE PROVISION*

William J. Mallett

INTRODUCTION

Growing demands on the transportation system and constraints on public resources have led to calls for more private sector involvement in the provision of highway and transit infrastructure through what are known as "public-private partnerships" (PPPs). The opportunity to own or lease assets that have the potential for generating stable, medium-level revenues over the long term has attracted private sector interest. According to the U.S. Department of Transportation "the term 'public-private partnership' is used for any scenario under which the private sector assumes a greater role in the planning, financing, design, construction, operation, and maintenance of a transportation facility compared to traditional procurement methods."[1] Typically the "public" in public-private partnerships refers to a state government, local government, or transit agency. The federal government, nevertheless, exerts influence over the prevalence and structure of PPPs through its transportation programs, funding, and regulatory oversight.

Proponents of PPPs argue that they are the best hope for injecting additional resources into the surface freight and passenger transportation systems for upkeep

---

* Excerpted from CRS Report Order Code RL34567, dated July 9, 2008.

and expansion. Furthermore, PPP proponents argue, private sector involvement often reduces costs, project delivery time, and public sector risk, and may improve project selection and project quality. Detractors, on the other hand, argue the potential for PPPs is limited, and that, unless carefully regulated, PPPs will disrupt the operation of the national surface transportation network, increase costs for the traveling public, and subvert the public planning process. With competing demands for public funds, there is also a concern that private funding will substitute for public resources with no net gain in transportation infrastructure.

A wide variety of public-private partnerships in highways and transit exist, but this chapter focuses on the two types of highway PPPs that are generating the most debate: (1) the leasing by the public sector to the private sector of *existing* infrastructure, sometimes referred to as "brownfield" facilities; and (2) the building, leasing, and owning of *new* infrastructure by private entities, sometimes known as "greenfield" facilities. A common, though not essential, element to greater private sector participation in highway infrastructure provision is the use of tolling. Vehicle tolls provide a revenue stream to retire bonds issued to finance a project and to provide a return on investment. Highway tolling can be implemented by public authorities, but it is widely believed that the privatization of transportation infrastructure will hasten the spread of tolling and may raise toll rates. Consequently, a discussion of PPPs must include, as this chapter does, the issue of vehicle tolling and other direct pricing mechanisms.

This chapter begins with a brief discussion of the surface transportation system and its financing needs as background to the debate on PPPs. That is followed by sections describing the different types of PPPs, with details of a few prominent examples, and the development of federal legislation with respect to PPPs. The chapter then discusses the main issues of contention with the construction and long-term leasing of highways by the private sector, particularly as they relate to the funding, planning, and operation of the surface transportation system, before providing some policy options Congress may wish to consider.

BACKGROUND

The appropriate role of the private sector in the provision of ostensibly public surface transportation infrastructure has been discussed for decades. But this debate has recently taken on a new urgency because of the magnitude of estimated future needs of the surface transportation system coupled with problems funding existing highway and transit programs at the federal, state, and local levels. A number of high profile PPP agreements, including the leasing of the Indiana Toll

Road and the Chicago Skyway described below, have also contributed to this heightened interest.

Although estimating future infrastructure needs is fraught with difficulty,[2] a number of recent reports have concluded that the nation's surface transportation infrastructure will require substantially more funding over the next few decades to deal with physical deterioration, congestion, and future demand for both passenger and freight travel.[3] Capital cost estimates prepared by the Department of Transportation (DOT), for example, suggest that the nation as a whole, including all levels of government and the private sector, needs to increase highway capital spending by 12% and transit capital spending by 25% from 2005 through 2024 in order to maintain the current condition and performance of the system.[4] Investment to improve conditions and performance would be higher than these estimates. The National Surface Transportation Policy and Revenue Study Commission (NSTPRSC), created under Section 1909 of the Safe, Accountable, Flexible, Efficient Transportation Equity Act — A Legacy for Users (P.L. 109-59; SAFETEA), estimated significantly greater needs than DOT in its report to Congress.[5] NSTPRSC's middle range capital spending estimate for highways by all levels of government and the private sector over the next 30 years (2006 through 2035), for instance, suggests an increase of between 96% and 176% over currently sustainable expenditures, and for transit the equivalent range is between 31% and 92%.[6]

At the same time that many argue for greater surface transportation infrastructure funding, there is concern that the main revenue mechanism at the federal level, the fuels tax, is faltering. The federal contribution to highway and transit infrastructure, approximately 40% of capital spending on these modes since the 1990s, is largely derived from the Highway Trust Fund which relies primarily on the federal fuels tax and less so on other vehicle-related taxes.[7] Almost all federal highway funds and approximately 80% of federal transit funds are derived from the trust fund. In its most recent estimates, the Congressional Budget Office (CBO) suggests that on its current path the Highway Account of the Highway Trust Fund will go into deficit sometime in FY2009, before the end of the current authorization period, and that the Mass Transit Account will go into deficit in FY20 12.[8]

Funding shortfalls in the Highway Trust Fund are related to a few key underlying factors, particularly the erosion of the real per gallon value of the fuels tax. The federal tax on gasoline was last raised in the early 1990s, by 5 cents in 1990 (P.L. 10 1-508) and then by 4.3 cents in 1993 (P.L. 103-66). Of the 5 cent increase in 1990, 2.5 cents was directed to the Highway Trust Fund and 2.5 cents was directed to the General Fund of the U.S. Treasury for deficit reduction, whereas in 1993 the entire 4.3 cents was directed to the General Fund for deficit reduction. The 2.5 cents increase in 1990 for deficit reduction was redirected to the Highway Trust Fund beginning October 1, 1995 with 2 cents going to the Highway Account and 0.5 cents to the Mass Transit Account (P.L. 103-66). The 4.3 cents raised in 1993 was redirected to the trust fund beginning October 1, 1997 with 3.44 cents going to the Highway Account and 0.86 cents to the Mass Transit Account (P.L. 105-34; P.L. 105-178). Consequently, the gasoline tax flowing to the Highway Trust Fund went from 9 cents to 11.5 cents per gallon in 1990, to 14 cents per gallon in 1995, and to 18.3 cents per gallon in 1997.

Adjusted for changes in the consumer price index (CPI), the federal tax on gasoline in 2006 was worth about 72% percent of its value in 1993.[9] Adjusted for changes in the price of materials used in highway construction, as estimated by FHWA, however, the federal gasoline tax was worth only 49% in 2006 compared with 1993.[10] Although the federal fuels tax in absolute terms has lost a good deal of its purchasing power since 1993, revenues to the trust fund in inflation-adjusted terms have not suffered as much because the amount of driving and, therefore, fuel consumption, has until recently continued to grow (see figure 1). Indeed, through the 1990s revenues continued to grow in real (inflation-adjusted) terms. However, revenues have been flat in real terms since at least 2001, and when adjusted for the price of highway construction materials fell sharply in both 2005 and 2006. For these reasons, many point to a disconnect between growing infrastructure needs on the one hand and the purchasing power of the revenues in the Highway Trust Fund on the other.

How the federal government ought to deal with the gap between revenues from traditional funding mechanisms, particularly the federal fuels tax, and future infrastructure investment needs is a major underlying issue in the debate about the role of PPPs. The two main sides of the debate were evident in the NSTPRSC report that contained both majority and minority views. The majority view, supported by nine of the twelve Commissioners, contended that severe underinvestment is the main problem facing transportation infrastructure in the years ahead. Expressing the desire for maintaining a strong federal role in financing the capital needs of the transportation system, at the aforementioned 40% level, they recommended a 25 to 40 cent-per-gallon increase in the federal fuels tax to be phased in over the next five years, and indexing the tax to inflation beginning in year 6, although, they argued, these increases need to be accompanied by major reforms of the federal program to make it more focused and efficient. The majority also argued that PPPs, private capital, and tolling, including congestion pricing, would need to be employed to a greater extent, but under a set of rules and regulations designed to protect the public interest.

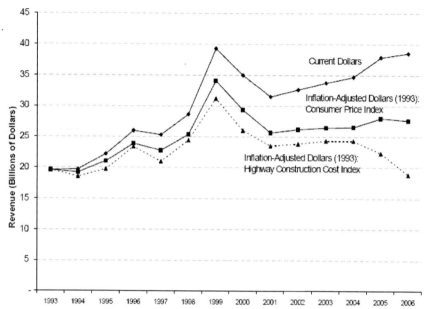

Sources: U.S. Department of Transportation, Federal Highway Administration, *Highway Statistics*, 2006 (Washington, DC); U.S. Department of Transportation, Federal Highway Administration, *Price Trends for Federal-Aid Highway Construction* (Washington, DC: 2008); and U.S. Department of Labor, Bureau of Labor Statistics, Consumer Price Index.

Figure 1. Total Highway Trust Fund Revenue, 1993-2006. (Current and Inflation-Adjusted 1993 Dollars).

An opposing viewpoint, expressed by three commissioners including the U.S. Secretary of Transportation Mary Peters, proposed that there is some need for additional resources in transportation infrastructure, but not to the extent estimated in the majority report. They argued that "a failure to properly align supply and demand, not a failure to generate sufficient tax revenues, is the essential policy failure" in transportation infrastructure provision.[11] A key ingredient of change, in their view, should be market-based reforms of highway systems allowing for much greater reliance on tolling, particularly congestion pricing, private sector participation, and, thus, PPPs. Moreover, they argue that the Federal role ought to be reduced and refocused in order to allow innovation at the state and local level.

TYPES OF TRANSPORTATION PUBLIC-PRIVATE PARTNERSHIPS

Public-private partnerships are typically conceived of as distinct from the traditional method of planning, building, operating, and maintaining highway and transit infrastructure. In the traditional method, known as "design, bid, build," the public sector decides there is a need for building a new facility, plans its development with a wide variety of community input, organizes the financing from tax revenue (either on a pay-as-you-go basis or through government bonds backed by tax revenue, tolls, or fares), lets out contracts to design and build the facility, and takes final ownership to operate and maintain the facility. In contrast, a public-private partnership involves more private sector participation in any or all phases of infrastructure development and operation. In many PPPs, private sector involvement is predicated on a revenue stream from the operation of a facility such as a vehicle toll or container fee.

According to the U.S. Department of Transportation, PPPs in highway and transit infrastructure provision can be categorized into six basic types, although the exact arrangements vary from project to project, many other types of PPPs are possible, and there is some overlap among types.[12] From least to most private responsibility, these six basic types of PPP are:

- *Private Contract Fee Services.* These types of PPPs turn over to the private sector more responsibility for providing services than is traditional. This may include contracting for operations and maintenance (O and M) services and program and financial management services. An example of this type of PPP is the partial outsourcing of street maintenance in the District of Columbia, including snow and ice removal.
- *Design-Build (DB).* This type of partnership arrangement combines two services that are traditionally separate, design and construction, into one fixed-fee contract. The public sector, nevertheless, retains ownership of the facility as well as responsibility for planning, preliminary engineering, financing, and O and M. An example of this type of PPP is the 12-mile light rail system in Minneapolis, Minnesota, opened in 2004, that was mostly constructed using two design-build contracts, one to construct the rail track and signal equipment and one for the trains.
- *Design-Build-Operate-Maintain (DBOM).* These partnerships go even further than design-build PPPs by adding private sector responsibility for

O and M once a facility goes into service. The public sector is still responsible for financing, and retains the risks and rewards associated with the operating costs and revenues. The 21- mile Hudson-Bergen light rail system in New Jersey is a good example of DBOM. The original fixed-price contract awarded to the 21st Century Rail Corporation in 1996 was for design and construction of the initial 10 miles by a guaranteed date and then 15 years of operation and maintenance. The contract was subsequently renegotiated for extensions to the system and to lengthen the O and M contract.

- *Long Term Lease Agreement.* This type of partnership typically involves the leasing of an existing facility to a private company for a specified amount of time. The private company usually pays an initial concession fee and must operate and maintain the facility to prescribed standards. The private company typically collects tolls on users and keeps the revenue to pay bond holders and to generate a return on its investment. Prominent examples of this type of PPP are the Chicago Skyway and the Indiana Toll Road (see descriptions below).

- *Design-Build-Finance-Operate (DBFO).* In addition to the designing, building, and operation of an infrastructure project, these types of PPPs also transfer to the private sector most of the financing responsibility. Debt financing leveraged with a revenue stream, such as tolls, is the most common mechanism in this type of PPP. However, financing may be supplemented with public sector grants and/or in-kind contributions such as right-of-way. The 14-mile Dulles Greenway toll road in northern Virginia is an example of this type of PPP.

- *Build-Own-Operate (BOO).* In this type of PPP, the public sector grants to the private sector the right to design, build, operate, maintain and own a facility in perpetuity. Consequently, conception of the project and subsequent planning is more likely to lay with the private sector. An example of this type of PPP is the 6 mile Foley Beach Express near Gulf Shores, Alabama that incorporates a toll bridge over the Intracoastal Waterway.

PROMINENT EXAMPLES OF
PUBLIC-PRIVATE PARTNERSHIPS

To illustrate the way in which PPPs can be structured, this section describes a few prominent examples, four dealing with highways and one dealing with transit. Two of the examples, the Chicago Skyway and Indiana Toll Road, both involve long-term leases of existing facilities, and have received a good deal of attention over the past few years. Both leasing deals have raised questions, among other things, about the loss of control of a major public asset for several generations, increases in toll rates, and the effects on the surrounding transportation network. Another example, the addition of High Occupancy Toll (HOT) Lanes to the Capital Beltway (I-495) in northern Virginia, involves private investment in new highway capacity that is seen by some as a boon to a state with limited public funding for major infrastructure projects. However, it too raises several public policy questions, including those about the public planning process for transportation infrastructure and the ability of lower-income travelers to pay tolls that may be high during the weekday morning and evening peak periods. The development of the Las Vegas Monorail provides an example of the potential and the difficulties of private investment in public transit. And the final example, the Missouri Safe and Sound program, details a plan for private involvement in repairing and maintaining a significant number of highway bridges. While innovative, the Missouri plan may commit a substantial amount of the state's federal bridge funding for 25 years, potentially tying the hands of future decision makers and reducing the flexibility of the state to react to other transportation challenges. The issues raised by these questions and several others are discussed in more depth in the "Issues for Congress" section later in this chapter.

Chicago Skyway

The Chicago Skyway is a 7.8 mile elevated toll road connecting the Dan Ryan Expressway (I-94) to the Indiana Toll Road (I-90). Built in 1958 without federal funds, the Skyway was operated and maintained by the City of Chicago Department of Streets and Sanitation until 2004 when it was leased for 99 years to the Skyway Concession Company (SCC), a private concessionaire that involves two well-known foreign companies involved in infrastructure investment, Cintra (Spain) and Macquarie Infrastructure Group (Australia). SCC won this concession with a bid of $1.83 billion in a competition that included four other detailed proposals. The City of Chicago and SCC signed a contract on October 27, 2004, and SCC began operating the Skyway on January 24, 2005. According to the lease agreement, SCC must operate and maintain the Skyway to certain standards, and, within limits, can collect and retain all toll revenue. For cars, tolls are limited to $2.50 through 2007, gradually rising to $5.00 in 2017. After that tolls can be increased by the greater of 2%, the percentage change in the CPI, or the percentage increase in per capita nominal GDP. Of the $1.83 billion collected by the City of Chicago, $463 million was used to repay the outstanding debt on the road, $392 million is being used to pay down the city's general obligation debt, and $875 million was placed into long-term and medium-term reserve funds.[13]

Indiana Toll Road

The Indiana Toll Road is a 157-mile segment carrying an Interstate designation that runs across northern Indiana linking with the Chicago Skyway in the west and the Ohio Turnpike in the east.[14] The Indiana Toll Road, built largely without federal funds and opened in 1956, was operated by the Indiana DOT from 1981 to 2006. After a bidding process involving eleven proposals, a 75-year lease concession was awarded to the Indiana Toll Road Concession Company (ITRCC), a partnership between Cintra and Macquarie Infrastructure Group, for $3.8 billion. ITRCC began operating the facility on June 29, 2006. For cars, tolls are limited to $8.00 through June 30, 2010. After that tolls can be increased by the greater of 2%, the percentage change in the CPI, or the percentage increase in per capita nominal GDP. The proceeds from the lease are being used by the Indiana DOT to fund 200 highway construction projects and 200 highway major preservation projects under the state's 10-year "Major Moves" initiative.[15] In addition, the 7 counties through which the toll road passes will receive payments of $40 million to $120 million for local transportation projects and all counties will receive extra state aid for transportation.

Northern Virginia I-495 HOT Lanes

In December 2007, the Virginia Department of Transportation (VDOT) signed an agreement with a private consortium to build and operate four new HOT lanes, two in each direction, on a 14-mile stretch of the Capital Beltway (I-495) from the Springfield Interchange to north of the Dulles Toll Road. The partnership between VDOT and the private consortium is an example of a Design-Build-Finance-Operate (DBFO) PPP. The new lanes will be operated using congestion pricing technology that collects a variable toll based on traffic levels. High-occupancy vehicles (HOV-3), motorcycles, buses, and emergency vehicles will travel without charge. The private consortium, Fluor Corporation and Transurban, is expected to finance all but $409 million of the estimated $1.9 billion project. The private consortium is committing $349 million in equity and will borrow the rest using Federal credit assistance, a Transportation Infrastructure Finance and Innovation Act (TIFIA) loan of $585 million and $586 million in tax-exempt private-activity bonds.[16] The contract is a fixed-price, fixed time, design-build contract, with an 80-year lease for operations, maintenance, and toll collection. Work to construct the new lanes began in the spring of 2008 and must be completed by spring 2013. The $409 million committed by the state will finance a number of additional highway improvements including the final phase of the Springfield Interchange, improvements to the I-66 interchange, reconstruction of some bridges on the Beltway, and participation in a regional congestion plan. The state will retain ownership of the new lanes and will share in toll revenues if they exceed an 8.1% return on investment. A similar project involving VDOT and Fluor-Transurban is being pursued on a 70 mile segment of I-395/I-95 from Arlington to Massaponax.[17]

Las Vegas Monorail

Possibly one of the most innovative PPPs in transit over the past few years has been the development of the Las Vegas Monorail system, currently a 4-mile system that connects hotels and other attractions on the Las Vegas Strip. Most transit PPPs have been of the design-build variety and a few have been design-build-operate-maintain, but direct government ownership and financial support has been an essential element of these types of projects. The Las Vegas Monorail, by contrast, has been more of a private venture, owned and operated by the Las Vegas Monorail Company, a non-profit corporation, financed with some tax-exempt bonds and an exemption from sales tax as a charitable organization.[18] The original segment of the system, operating between two major hotels, was opened in 1995. The system was expanded in 2004 with financial and in-kind contributions from hotels and resorts in addition to the sale of tax-exempt bonds that are being repaid with passenger fares and advertising revenues.[19] A proposal to extend the system to McCarren International Airport was approved by Clarke County in November 2006. Despite this approval, the project does not appear to have attracted the approximately $500 million needed to finance construction.[20] Financial problems with the existing system may be to blame. Recent newspaper reports have stated that the system is failing to meet its operating and debt expenses by about $30 million annually and that the company may exhaust its reserve funds by 2010.[21] One estimate suggests that while the monorail carried about 22,000 passengers a day in late 2007, it needs to carry about 35,000 a day to break even.[22]

Missouri DOT Safe and Sound Program

Another innovative PPP is the Safe and Sound Program proposed by Missouri Department of Transportation (MoDOT).[23] Under this program, MoDOT is seeking a private sector partner to repair 802 state bridges by 2012 and then to maintain them in good condition for another 25 years. MoDOT estimates the state has about 10,000 bridges, of which about 1,000 are rated in poor or serious condition.[24] In exchange for financing the repair and maintenance costs, beginning in 2012, the private partner will receive regular payments from the state for the remaining 25 years. The state is proposing to use federal bridge program funds to make the payments. The state has called this type of PPP, Design-Build-Finance-Maintain, the bridge equivalent of the Design-Build-Finance-Operate model described above. The state received two bids for the contract and chose Missouri Bridge Partners, a consortium of firms including Zachry American Infrastructure, Parsons Transportation Group, Fred Weber Inc., Clarkson Construction, HNTB, and Infrastructure Corporation of America. MoDOT estimates that the project will cost between $400 million and $600 million. Although it is not yet clear how the project will be financed, in 2007, the U.S. Department of Transportation approved a $700 million allocation of Private Activity Bonds to the MoDOT for the project.[25]

FEDERAL LEGISLATION AND PUBLIC-PRIVATE PARTNERSHIPS

In the period from the mid-1950s through the 1970s, highway and transit infrastructure provision were both marked by a large infusion of public funding, particularly from the federal government.[26] Highway spending grew from the mid-1950s, in large part to finance the construction of the Interstate Highway System, whereas transit spending grew from the mid-1960s with the public sector takeover of struggling private transit companies and an investment in new vehicles and infrastructure. During this period, the private sector's role was largely limited to bidding on and building what the public sector had planned, designed, and financed, a process known as "design-bid-build". With the effective completion of the Interstates by the early 1980s, however, public capital spending on highways had already declined in real terms, and the federal share of total public capital spending that had reached highs in the late 1970s and early 1980s began to decline.[27] Transit spending by all levels of government, that had grown rapidly in the 1970s, slowed dramatically in the 1980s and the Federal share declined.[28]

According to some analysts, these trends spurred interest in the use of public-private partnerships, as states and localities, particularly those in fast growing parts of the country, searched for new ways to fund and build transportation infrastructure.[29] In highway transportation during the 1 980s, there was some renewed focus on vehicle tolling, a potential revenue stream that was of interest to private investors as well as public authorities. Consequently, by the late 1980s, spurred on by experience in other parts of the world and developments in automated toll collection technology, seven states had approved legislation to allow private investment in highway projects.[30] Two of the earliest projects developed under these new rules were the Dulles Greenway in Virginia and SR-91 in California, toll roads that both opened in 1995. According to DOT, 23 states currently have PPP enabling legislation.[31]

In transit, new revenue was sought from the development of new private facilities on or over transit agency land, a process known as joint development.[32] For example, joint development was used in the construction of mixed-use facilities (offices, retail, and a hotel) surrounding the Washington Metropolitan Area Transit Authority's (WMATA) Bethesda, MD station completed in 1985. The air-rights lease for this development generates $1.6 million annually in rents for WMATA.[33]

Highway Public-Private Partnerships

With the growing interest in tolling and public-private partnerships, the federal government in the late 1980s began to explore the possibilities for their inclusion in federal surface transportation programs. The three main areas of legislative change to accommodate this in the highway program have been in the areas of highway tolling, innovative finance, and innovative contracting.

Highway Tolling

Since the passage of the Intermodal Surface Transportation Efficiency Act of 1991 (ISTEA; P.L. 102-240), it has generally been permissible to use tolling to finance the construction or reconstruction of federally supported roads, tunnels, and bridges, except on the Interstate system, even when the facility is privately owned (23 U.S.C. § 129(a)).[34] Moreover, over the years, and particularly since the late 1980s, Congress has created a number of exceptions to tolling restrictions on Interstates that permit the development of PPPs. In the Surface Transportation and Uniform Relocation Assistance Act of 1987 (P.L. 100-17), Congress established a pilot program allowing federal funds to be used, with a maximum federal share of 35%, in the construction or reconstruction of up to seven toll facilities. However, these new or reconstructed facilities had to be publicly owned and operated and Interstate highways were specifically excluded. In the next authorization bill, ISTEA, Congress removed the pilot program status, allowed states to convert non-tolled roads, bridges, and tunnels to tolled facilities, raised the federal share to 50%, and allowed for private ownership and operation. ISTEA also established the Congestion Pricing Pilot Program which allowed federal funds to be used in the implementation of congestion pricing (variable tolls) on up to 5 projects, of which a maximum of 3 could be Interstates.

The Congestion Pricing Pilot Program was continued in the Transportation Equity Act for the 21st Century (TEA-21; P.L. 105-178), enacted in 1998, but expanded to allow 15 projects and renamed the Value Pricing Pilot Project. Additionally, TEA-21 created another pilot program, the Interstate System Reconstruction and Rehabilitation Pilot Program, for up to 3 toll projects with the purpose of reconstruction on the Interstate Highway System. To date, a decade later, only two of the three slots have been filled, with I-70 in Missouri and I-81 in Virginia having been granted approval.

Most recently, in SAFETEA, Congress authorized three new ways to institute tolling on federally funded roads and modified another method.[35] Section 1121 of SAFETEA amended 23 U.S.C. § 166 to allow conversion of High Occupancy Vehicle (HOV) lanes to High Occupancy Toll (HOT) lanes. SAFETEA also created two new programs, the Express Lane Demonstration program (Section 1604(b)) and the Interstate System Construction Toll Pilot program (Section 1604(c)). The Express Lane Demonstration program authorizes up to 15 new tolled facilities from the conversion of existing HOV facilities or where new lanes are constructed. The program explicitly provides for private investment. The Interstate System Construction Toll Pilot program authorizes tolling on the construction of three new Interstate highways. To date, one of the three slots has been reserved for construction of I-73 in South Carolina, although the slot applies to I-73 in other states as well if they want to construct their portion of it under this program. SAFETEA also extended and modified the Value Pricing Pilot Program by setting aside a portion of the authorized funding for congestion pricing pilot projects that do not involve highway tolls, such as parking pricing strategies and pay-as-you drive pricing involving innovative forms of car ownership and insurance.[36]

Although it is not entirely clear what effect the changes in federal law have had on the development of toll roads, a substantial number of projects have been initiated since the passage of ISTEA, and this activity appears to have accelerated. A recent survey sponsored by the Federal Highway Administration found that since the passage of ISTEA, a total of 168 toll road projects were initiated in 27 states and one U.S. territory.[37] These projects totaled 3,770 centerline miles and 14,560 lane miles of highway, although not all the projects involved new capacity. About one-third of the new toll lane-miles were on the Interstate system, and about one-half of the toll roads developed since ISTEA involved a public-private partnership. Of the 168 toll road projects, 50 were open at the time of the survey in 2005. The data also indicate that about 50 to 75 miles of toll roads were developed annually in the decade after the passage of ISTEA in 1991, and that more recently this has increased to about 150 miles annually.

Innovative Finance

Another way in which changes in federal law have encouraged PPPs is through developments in innovative financing, a term that covers a broad set of ways to finance infrastructure outside the usual methods involving pay- as-you-go (direct appropriations), intergovernmental grants, and government revenue bonds.[38] In ISTEA, Congress approved some new concepts in infrastructure financing particularly in the use of user fees. This led to the creation in 1994 of the Innovative Finance Test and Evaluation (TE-045) program that sought to implement and evaluate some new financing tools in the federal-aid highway program. Some of the ideas developed in this experimental program were subsequently enacted in The National Highway System Designation Act of 1995 (P.L. 104-59) including the State Infrastructure Bank (SIB) pilot program that permitted certain states to set up revolving funds with federal money, with the intent of leveraging other public and private resources for infrastructure projects.

Another major development came in the form of the Transportation Infrastructure Finance and Innovation Act (TIFIA) of 1998, a part of TEA-21 that created a program for federal credit assistance on major transportation projects. TIFIA funding is designed to leverage non-federal funding including investment from the private sector, and as originally conceived was for projects costing at least $100 million (or at least $30 million in the case of Intelligent Transportation Systems (ITS) projects). TIFIA financing authorized under TEA-21 was extended by SAFETEA and modified by permitting all public-private partnerships to apply directly, expanding eligibility to freight rail and intermodal facilities, and by lowering the eligibility threshold to $50 million in general and to $15 million in the case of ITS projects.[39]

SAFETEA also added to the federal tax code several private transportation activities as eligible for federally tax-exempt state and local bond financing. According to federal tax law, state and local bonds are classified as either governmental bonds or private activity bonds. Government bonds are those issued to finance public activities, such as building a school, and private activity bonds are those issued to finance activities that are less public in nature, such as an investor owned water utility. In general, the interest on government bonds is exempt from federal tax, whereas interest on private activity bonds is taxable. A tax-exempt bond can be issued at a lower interest rate and, therefore, provides cheaper financing for a project than a taxable bond. Over the years, some types of private activities for which state and local bonds are issued have been afforded tax-exempt status.[40] These private activities are known as "qualified private activities." Prior to SAFETEA, a number of transportation facilities were classified in the tax code as qualified private activities. These included airports, docks and wharves, mass commuting facilities, and high-speed intercity rail facilities. Title XI, Section 1143 of SAFETEA added qualified highway and surface freight transfer facilities.

In addition to limiting the type of private activities eligible for tax-exempt financing, Congress has also typically placed a limit on the amount of such bonds that can be issued. Section 1143 of SAFETEA, therefore, also included a $15 billion limit on the bonds that could be issued for qualified highway or surface freight transfer facilities, although bonds issued under this section are exempt from the state volume caps that exist for the general issuance of private activity bonds. Under the law, the Secretary of Transportation is charged with deciding on bond allocations.

Despite the general expansion of tax-exempt bond financing, some have questioned its cost effectiveness and have suggested that traditional federal grants or carefully designed tax-credit bonds would provide the same amount of federal subsidy at a lower overall cost to the U.S. Treasury.[41]

Innovative Contracting

Another area in which the federal government has increasingly encouraged private participation in highway infrastructure is in contracting and project delivery. FHWA began experimenting with innovative contracting under Special Experiment Project 14 (SEP-14) and Special Experiment Project 15 (SEP-15). SEP-14, begun in 1990, focused primarily on four methods of innovative contracting: cost-plus-time bidding, lane rental arrangements, warranties, and design-build contracts. SEP-15, begun in 2004, focuses on project delivery in the areas of contracting, compliance with environmental regulations, right-of-way acquisition, and project finance.[42]

With a number of successes, legislation followed to make several of these innovations mainstream methods for delivering infrastructure projects. One of the most important of these for public-private partnerships, design-build contracting, was made a permissible method of contracting in the federal-aid highway program in

1998 (by Section 1307 of TEA-21), albeit with certain conditions. These conditions included limiting design-build contracting to projects over $50 million or over $5 million on ITS projects, and restricting the commencement of final design until after meeting NEPA requirements. In 2005, Congress eliminated the $50 million floor for design-build contracts and permitted agencies to enter into contracts with private sector firms before NEPA approval. This allows private sector involvement at an earlier stage than previously allowed. In 2005, Congress also enacted a 180-day limitation on the time for challenging federal approvals, including environmental approvals, aimed at reducing the risk for projects, a provision that is particularly important for project revenue financed projects.[43]

Transit Public-Private Partnerships

In transit, the use of, and interest in, public-private partnerships has been somewhat more limited. Most likely this is because most transit projects are revenue negative, that is they require some kind of ongoing financial support in addition to passenger fares and other system-related revenues. Nevertheless, there have been a number of federal legislative and regulatory initiatives encouraging private sector involvement in transit, particularly in financing and contracting.

Innovative Financing

One of the earliest legislative initiatives in the realm of innovative financing with implications for private sector involvement in transit can be found in certain provisions of the National Urban Mass Transportation Act of 1974 (P.L. 93-503). The act permitted federal assistance for joint development projects, projects that typically involved the commercial or residential development of land on or near transit stations.[44] These types of projects, however, were discouraged by an administrative decision by the Urban Mass Transportation Administration (now know as the Federal Transit Administration or FTA) in the 1980s that federal subsidies could only be used to defray project costs after taking into account contributions from private partners, effectively substituting private dollars for federal dollars. But FTA's policy on joint development was revised again in 1997, as directed by Congress in ISTEA, to allow land acquired with federal funding to be used in joint development projects and income derived from such projects to be used for transit operation.[45] TEA-21 then made joint development eligible for reimbursement in federal transit grant programs by incorporating such activities into the definition of a transit capital project.[46] The law pertaining to joint development was last modified by SAFETEA, with regulations promulgated in 2007. Among other things, SAFETEA added intercity bus and rail terminals as permitted uses for joint development authority.[47]

Innovative Contracting

In the realm of innovative contracting, ISTEA furthered the use of PPPs in transit by initiating a demonstration program to explore the use of DB/DBOM in the New Starts program. FTA picked five projects to be a part of the demonstration program: Los Angeles Union Station Intermodal Terminal, Baltimore Light Rail Transit System Extensions, San Juan Tren Urbano, Bay Area Rapid Transit (BART) Airport Extension, and Northern New Jersey Hudson Bergen LRT. ISTEA also directed FTA to issue guidance on the use of DB/DBOM in the Federal New Starts program. More recently, Section 3011(c) of SAFETEA authorized the Secretary of Transportation to establish a pilot program to explore the use of PPPs in new fixed-guideway capital projects (transit rail or BRT) involving federal funds. This new program is known as the Public-Private Partnership Pilot Program, or "Penta-P." To date, FTA has invited applications from interested state and local authorities for inclusion in the pilot program, and has selected two rail projects in Denver, CO and two BRT projects in Houston, TX.

ISSUES FOR CONGRESS

The two main issues for Congress with regard to public-private partnerships in surface transportation are: (1) the extent to which PPPs can be relied upon to meet the future resource needs of the surface transportation system; and (2) the effects of long-term highway concessions on the operation and planning of the surface transportation system. Some of the specific issues raised in transportation operations include the effects of PPPs on national uniformity in highway operation, interstate commerce, the mobility of low-income households, and traffic diversion. Issues raised in transportation planning include non-compete provisions in PPP lease agreements, unsolicited proposals, lease duration, and foreign control of transportation assets. Each of these is discussed below, as is the issue of identifying and protecting the public interest in general. This section begins with an evaluation of the place of PPPs in the funding of surface transportation infrastructure.

Additional Resources for Transportation Infrastructure

One of the main attractions of PPPs, according to advocates, is that they provide additional resources for the provision of transportation infrastructure. Some advocates of PPPs argue that without additional sources of investment the nation risks undermining the transportation system as a result of physical deterioration and congestion. Primarily these additional resources are associated with a project-related revenue stream such as vehicle tolls, container fees, or, in the case of transit station development, building rents. Private sector resources may come from an initial payment to lease an existing asset in exchange for future revenue, as with the Indiana Toll Road and Chicago Skyway, or it may involve developing an asset along with a new revenue stream. Either way, a facility user fee is often the key to unlocking private sector participation and resources.

Of course, the public sector can build toll roads, raise tolls on existing facilities, or, in some cases, even institute tolls on existing "free" roads, bridges, and tunnels when reconstructing or replacing the facility. Proponents of PPPs argue, however, that for two primary reasons the private sector can attract more capital to highway infrastructure than the public sector.[48] First, a privately operated toll road can be financed with both debt (bond) and equity financing, and that because equity investors have an opportunity to share in the profits, they tend to be less conservative than traditional municipal bond investors. In addition, private concessions are often for terms longer than traditional municipal bond maturities of 25, 30, or 40 years, hence, with an income stream over a longer period the concessionaire can raise extra capital. Based on these principles, one estimate suggests that the $1.83 billion raised in the 99-year concession of the Chicago Skyway, would only have raised $800 billion in traditional bond financing.[49]

Second, PPP proponents argue that toll facilities are less successful when operated by the public sector because political forces typically make it difficult to raise tolls in line with costs. Not only does this create a potential further drag on public coffers in the future, it also affects the ability of government to borrow money to initiate construction. By contrast, it is sometimes argued, the private sector can generate the necessary funds because lenders are more sure that toll revenues will be stable when decisions are made primarily on a business rationale.[50] An exception to the difference between the public and private sector in setting toll rates is the use of dynamic tolling in congestion pricing schemes in which the toll is adjusted up and down to maintain "free-flowing" traffic. In such cases, traffic demand determines the price. Moreover, in leasing agreements, the toll rate is often regulated, thus the private operator does not have complete freedom to choose when and by how much to raise the toll. Nevertheless, proponents of private sector involvement argue "long-term toll road concessions...are not simply a private-sector version of a public-sector toll agency. They are a new and important innovation in U.S. highway finance."[51]

The Secretary of Transportation Mary Peters has repeatedly stated that there is at least $400 billion of private sector capital available for infrastructure investment.[52] One independent review of the evidence has suggested that this is a credible number, even taking into account the current problems in global credit markets, with funds available ranging from $340 billion to $600 billion.[53] However, this $400 billion of private capital is available to be invested anywhere in the world and in any type of infrastructure,[54] casting some doubt on how much realistically might be available to be invested in highways and transit in the United States.[55] It is also unclear over what period of time the $400 billion is available for investment, and how much more might be available once that amount is committed. Nevertheless, supporters say even a portion of this potential investment capital would provide a significant boost to U.S. highways and transit infrastructure. DOT's current estimate of capital spending by all levels of government to maintain current highway conditions and performance over the next 20 years is $78.8 billion annually, $8.5 billion more than is currently being spent. In transit, spending needs are estimated to be $15.8 billion annually, $3.2 billion more than is currently being spent.[56]

While most agree that PPPs will likely attract new private capital to transportation infrastructure provision, some argue that the scale of this capital is likely to be relatively modest when viewed in the context of total highway and transit infrastructure spending.[57] The American Association of State Highway and Transportation Officials (AASHTO) notes, for example, that highway tolling, either public or private, currently accounts for approximately 5% of highway revenues and optimistically will meet 7% to 9% of future national investment needs.[58] Because transit is revenue negative, it is likely that transit PPPs could never generate anywhere near this share of investment. This suggests that when considering the future needs of both highway and transit infrastructure nationally, PPPs are likely to generate somewhat less than this estimated level of 7% to 9%.

A related point, and one not fully considered in these estimates, however, is that the institution of a toll not only provides revenue to improve the supply of infrastructure, but also tends to suppress and/or divert travel demand. With limited toll road mileage, this effect may be relatively minor and may be more likely to result in traffic diversion (see below). Widespread tolling, on the other hand, may result not in route diversion, but in travelers switching to other modes, changing the time of a trip to avoid a charge, or foregoing travel altogether. DOT has made a preliminary attempt to estimate, theoretically, the effects of universal congestion pricing on infrastructure demand, and suggests they would be substantial. As noted earlier, DOT's current estimate of the annual cost to maintain highway and bridges over 20 years from 2005 through 2024 is $78.8 billion a year (in 2004 dollars), $8.5 billion more than the $70.3 billion spent in 2004 by all levels of government. Under the universal congestion pricing scenario, DOT's preliminary estimate of capital spending needs over 20 years shrinks to $57.2 billion, $21.6 billion less than its estimate of capital needs, and $13.1 billion less than is currently being spent.[59] Of course, there is little likelihood that such widespread highway pricing could be instituted anytime soon, nor do DOT's estimates include the administrative and startup costs that would be involved, or the technical difficulties of such as plan. DOT's analysis is also silent on the effects of universal congestion pricing on the demand for other modes of passenger and freight travel, such as public transit and freight rail. Nevertheless, the research does indicate that direct user fees, such as congestion pricing, may reduce the demand for new highway infrastructure.

Diversion of Resources from the Transportation Sector

Another concern in the transportation sector is that the resources generated from transportation PPPs will not be used to finance transportation infrastructure needs. State and local governments have significant demands for funding in many different areas. Asset leases in particular provide a mechanism to generate large sums of money that could be used to fund a wide range of social services. That is why some have argued that unlike concessions in the provision of new toll roads that are "added value," the leasing of existing roads might be considered "revenue extraction."[60] This concern has been realized in the case of the Chicago Skyway, discussed earlier, as some of the lease payment has been used for non-transportation purposes. The City of Chicago, however, has noted that, among other things, it has created a reserve fund that generates in interest revenue what the road did in toll revenue, and that excess toll revenues from the Skyway were previously directed to the city's general fund.[61] The GAO has stated that the city's credit rating improved when it reduced its general obligation debt, thereby reducing the future cost of borrowing.[62] The possibility remains, nevertheless, that the money generated by asset leases may end up being used for current transportation and non-transportation needs and that future facility users, in some cases three or four generations from now, may end up paying higher tolls as a result.[63]

Diversion of resources may also be of more general concern in that new private resources attracted to transportation infrastructure may substitute for public resources in the sector, not add to them. With competing demands for public funds, it is possible that with increases in private funding, state and local governments will divert public resources to other deserving public programs with no net gain in transportation infrastructure. In a study of the effect of federal highway funding increases on state highway funding between 1982 and 2002, GAO observed a substitution effect, particularly between 1998 and 2002 when a 40% increase in federal capital spending was accompanied by a 4% drop in state and local capital spending.[64]

Other Resource Benefits

As well as the potential for additional capital, PPPs may also generate new resources for transportation infrastructure in at least two other ways. First, PPPs may improve resource efficiency through improved management and innovation in construction, maintenance, and operation, in effect providing more infrastructure for the same price. PPP proponents argue that private companies are more able to examine the full life-cycle cost of investments, whereas public agency decisions are often tied to short-term budget cycles. In the case of the Hudson-Bergen Light Rail in New Jersey, procured under a DBOM contract, DOT estimates that the project saved 30% over the more traditional design-bid-build procurement method, a saving of about $345 million.[65] Skeptics point out, however, that these savings may not materialize if the public sector has to spend a substantial amount of time on procurement, oversight, and disputes that may result in litigation. For example, the California DOT has had a number of costly disputes with its private partners.[66] Furthermore, GAO argues that most state governments do not have the necessary capacity to manage these contracts.[67]

Second, through PPPs the private sector may bear many of the financial risks that exist with building, maintaining, and operating infrastructure. Risks abound in the development and operation of infrastructure, including the risk that construction and maintenance will cost more and/or take longer than foreseen. Another risk with toll facilities is that once built there will be less demand than estimated. Transferring these risks to the private sector, according to proponents, will save public agencies significant amounts of money, particularly as cost and schedule overruns are common with transportation infrastructure projects. Detractors argue that in some cases this transfer of risk may prove illusory as major miscalculations may force the public sector to assume project ownership. Consequently, this line of reasoning goes, PPPs may in fact be false partnerships in that profits will be retained in the private sector, while major losses will be borne by the public sector.[68] Moreover, as the GAO points out, not all the risks can or should be shifted to the private sector. For instance, a major risk associated with transportation infrastructure projects that the private sector is unlikely to be able to accept is the delay and uncertainty associated with the environmental review process.[69]

Effects of Public-Private Partnerships on the Operation and Planning of the Surface Transportation System

The other main issue that may be of interest to Congress is the effects of PPPs on the planning and operation of surface transportation system, particularly the highway network. This has been expressed by some as identifying and protecting the "public interest" in transportation infrastructure.[70]

Operation of the Highway Network

One of the main concerns of the critics of public-private partnerships in highways is that it will create a patchwork of tolled and non-tolled roads, undermining national uniformity in highway operation, increasing travel costs (see below), and ultimately impeding passenger travel and interstate commerce.[71] Conceivably, this perceived "patchwork" will add a good deal of complexity to everyday routing decisions, and possibly longer term location decisions, that may mean the cheapest route is no longer the shortest, quickest route. The American Trucking Associations (ATA) has also expressed the concern that tolling and privatization will place an extra administrative burden on national and regional trucking companies because of having to do business with a multitude of public and private tolling entities.[72] Others are concerned that the first facilities to be candidates for leasing will be those that serve a high proportion of users from other states or local jurisdictions.[73]

In response, proponents of PPPs argue that the national highway system is already a complex network of tolled and non-tolled facilities owned and operated by a multitude of different public authorities and private companies, and that private highway operators have a financial incentive to ensure efficient operations. Moreover, as noted earlier, some PPP advocates argue that without additional sources of investment the nation risks undermining the network as a result of physical deterioration and congestion.[74]

Highway Travel Costs

Probably of greatest concern to many users of the highway system is that greater private sector involvement will lead to substantial increases in travel costs through the proliferation of tolled roads and toll rates that will rise more quickly than has typically been the case under public control. This is of particular concern where no new service is provided, such as a new facility or the addition of new lanes on an existing facility, and where there is no viable, non-tolled alternative. Proponents of PPPs agree that private sector participation will most likely lead to an increase in direct highway user costs, but note that this is the price to be paid for not providing highway infrastructure through taxation. Morever, proponents agree that tolls on privately operated toll roads are likely to increase more than those on publicly operated roads. Supporters of PPPs argue that is not because private operators charge too much, but that public operators tend to charge too little because increasing tolls in line with inflation and other costs is politically difficult.

Of particular concern to critics of privately operated toll roads is any situation where there is no viable travel alternative, or to put it another way, where the private road operator has significant monopoly power. In such a situation, these critics argue that, unless carefully regulated, toll rates can be set very high and the rate of return on investment will be unreasonably large. ATA has expressed such concerns about toll rates on the Indiana Toll Road, a part of the country where no alternative travel route exists. PPP proponents argue that concession agreements typically cap toll rates in line with growth factors in the broader economy. Moreover, they argue that a concessionaire is unlikely to set rates at a level that reduces traffic to a level that will cause its revenue to drop.[75]

Traffic Diversion

Another concern with the network effects of PPPs, and tolling in general, is that it has the potential for diverting traffic on to other routes, possibly increasing congestion, contributing to possible roadway deterioration, and reducing safety. Private control, it is argued, will lead to higher toll rates and, therefore, more diversion.[76] Diversion of truck traffic is seen as particularly problematic, although diversion of all types of vehicles may occur. A recent study suggests that the safety impacts and infrastructure damage resulting from diversion may be substantial, although the scale of effects will vary by route and the size of the toll.[77] For example, it has been noted that because there is no viable alternative, increased tolls on the Indiana Toll Road associated with its leasing are not likely to impose costs on the surrounding routes and jurisdictions. Proponents of PPPs argue that although some diversion may occur, it is in the private toll operator's interest to provide a service that will attract vehicles.

Equity

Critics of PPPs argue that new or higher highway tolls discriminate against low income drivers who will be forced to use alternative routes, other means of travel, or to forego travel altogether. The concern is that there will be one segment of the highway network providing a high quality of service for those able and willing to pay and another segment of the highway network with poor quality of service for those unable or unwilling to pay. Proponents of PPPs argue that many income groups stand to benefit from highways with a better level of service and point to surveys of users on toll roads such as SR-91 that show a significant level of usage by people from low income households.[78] Tolls, nevertheless, still place a greater burden on lower-income than higher-income households, but some argue that tolls may be less of a burden on lower-income households than extra fuel, sales, and property taxes.[79]

Infrastructure Planning

The network effects of some highway PPPs, as discussed above, are consequences that might ensue in the short to medium term. However, these same type of PPPs may also have a longer term effect on the network as a result of their influence on decisions about what to build and where, that is the infrastructure planning process. Proponents of PPPs argue that private sector investment not only will generate more resources for transportation, but will result in resources being committed to the most effective projects. It is frequently argued that because of the political process, government funding of transportation infrastructure is spread too widely, or worse, is spent on cost-ineffective projects. A number of studies have shown, for example, that geographic equity is often a basis for distributing transportation funding and selecting projects.[80] Private sector investments on the other hand, it is argued, would focus on projects that have the greatest potential economic returns. Foremost among these are congestion relief projects in places where demand is significantly greater than supply.

Skeptics, on the other hand, point out that one possible problem with relying on private investment to fund infrastructure development, maintenance, and operation is that large parts of the highway network carry relatively few vehicles and are unlikely to attract much interest from the private sector. These types of PPPs, therefore, are unlikely to address transportation issues in rural areas, issues that are often focused on connectivity, maintenance, and safety. The hope among proponents is that relieved of responsibility by the private sector for some parts of the heavily traveled network, the public sector can concentrate on other parts of the network. Conceivably, however, relying much more heavily on PPPs may eventually disrupt the transportation network by directing too few resources to links that carry relatively little traffic but provide important connections between the more heavily traveled segments.

Unsolicited Proposals

One of the ways in which concerns about the planning effects of PPPs have surfaced is over whether or not a state will accept unsolicited proposals. It is generally assumed that projects for which proposals are solicited from the private sector will have come through the public planning process. Unsolicited project proposals, on the other hand, are those initiated by the private sector and may or may not reflect the priorities of the state, region, or locality as contained in short and long-range plans. Consequently, some have suggested that state PPP enabling legislation should not permit unsolicited proposals. Proponents of PPPs argue that this would stifle innovative ideas, and that while a proposal may be unsolicited, to come to fruition it would have to pass through the public review process.

Non-Compete Provisions

Another possible effect on the transportation system is that some PPP contracts restrict what types of improvements can be made near a privately operated facility. In some cases, the private sector partner has insisted on a non-compete clause restricting nearby improvements with the potential for reducing traffic on the privately operated facility, or, if they are made, providing compensation. Some have argued that these non-compete clauses impede the ability of public agencies to increase capacity and their ability to devise coordinated congestion management policies.[81] Proponents of PPPs argue that there must be some protection from unlimited competition of "free-roads" provided by the taxpayer, otherwise it would be very difficult to secure private sector involvement. However, some proponents argue that agreements need to strike the right balance between protecting the private sector interest and the public interest in mobility and choice. Consequently, concession agreements "seldom, if ever, ban all 'free road' additions near the toll road. And they usually provide for compensation for reduced traffic, rather than forbidding public-sector roadway additions."[82]

Lease Duration

Another effect on the transportation network, some argue, may result from the very long-term nature of some lease agreements. Terms on recent leases include 90 years for the Chicago Skyway, 75 years for the Indiana Toll Road, and 80 years for the northern Virginia HOT lanes. PPP proponents argue that long time horizons are needed to generate the returns necessary to compensate for the risks. One concern is that this will tie the hands of policymakers for generations. Another concern with the leasing of existing facilities and the payment of an up-front concession fee is that future users may have to pay higher tolls to finance current spending. Consequently, some have suggested that agreements should be relatively short, and, as a general rule, should not extend beyond the design-life of a facility. PPP proponents, on the other hand, argue that concession agreements typically include provisions that allow for reasonable amendments and for third-party arbitration of disagreements.[83]

Foreign Control

Another concern of some opponents of PPPs is that they often result in a concession controlled by a foreign company. The predominant reason for this is that PPPs are more prevalent in other countries, particularly France, Spain, and Australia, hence, there are more companies from these countries that have experience with such transactions. Critics charge that this control might impede national security in an emergency and that the profits will go to foreign investors. Proponents of PPPs point out that there is no more risk to the United States from foreign-owned companies than domestic ones. After all, they argue, these foreign companies are willing to invest their money in an immovable asset. Proponents argue that this is a good thing because it shows foreign investors have confidence in the economic, political, and legal environment of the United States.

Protecting the Public Interest

In a study of PPPs in highway infrastructure provision, the Government Accountability Office (GAO) states that these institutional arrangements offer a number of benefits for states and localities but also present a number of trade-offs and potential problems. They identify a number of benefits such as the building of new facilities without using public funds and more efficient operations, among others. They also identify the trade-offs and problems with PPPs such as possible higher toll rates and lack of public control. As a result, the GAO argues that, as with any highway project, there is not one easily identifiable "public interest" but multiple stakeholders with overlapping interests that must be weighed against each other. They note, to date, that protecting the public interest in PPPs has been done on a project-by-project basis through the terms of concession agreements. They suggest that a more systematic approach to identifying and evaluating the public interest in PPPs be developed and employed, as has been done in other countries such as Australia. They suggest that the federal government needs to identify and evaluate the *national* public interest in highway projects that employ a PPP.[84]

POLICY OPTIONS FOR CONGRESS

There are at least three broad policy options that Congress could consider in the formation and operation of PPPs in surface transportation infrastructure delivery: (1) to continue with the current policy of incremental changes and experimentation in program incentives and regulation; (2) to actively encourage PPPs with program incentives, but with relatively tight regulatory controls; and (3) to aggressively encourage the use of PPPs through program incentives and deregulation in the areas of tolling, contracting, and financing. It should be pointed out that at the level of detailed policy prescriptions these three options are not necessarily mutually exclusive, as Congress could decide to deregulate in one area while enhancing regulation in another, and may add funding to one program and cut funding to another. For example, Congress might decide to do away with regulations in the construction and operation of new highway capacity and at the same time develop tighter regulations in the leasing of existing highways. Nevertheless, these three broad policy options provide an overall framework for Congressional action on PPPs.

The first broad policy option is to essentially carry on the path that has been followed over the past few authorizations, one of incremental changes and experimentation. As part of such a policy, Congress may opt to generally reauthorize the existing programs and retain existing regulatory controls. This cautious approach might avoid the major pitfalls of private sector involvement, but would likely mean slower growth in toll revenue and private equity investment than more aggressive approaches to the development of PPPs. Consequently this approach would require substantial reliance on other funding mechanisms. Some minor changes to existing programs and regulations might include expanding the number of available slots in the Interstate System Construction Toll Pilot program from the three currently permitted, and continuing and expanding the Penta-P program in transit.

A second option for Congress would be to more aggressively promote the use of PPPs, particularly certain types, but with a set of new regulations designed to protect the public interest from their perceived problems. This option might be considered a federally directed program of PPP development, and is an approach broadly similar to the one advocated by the majority report of the NSTPRSC.

The NSTPRSC report argues that Congress should encourage the use of tolling, congestion pricing, and PPPs, but with a number of conditions and restrictions. The NSTPRSC proposes that states and their partners be given the authority to variably toll new capacity on the Interstate system as a way to fund construction and to better manage the new lanes. They also suggest that authority be given to implement congestion pricing on new and existing Interstates in metropolitan areas with a population of one million or more. The Commission argues that for proposals concerning tolling and pricing on the Interstates, Congress should set up an approval process with strict criteria that includes requirements that: revenue be used only for transportation improvements in the same corridor; rates be set to avoid discrimination against certain types of travelers such as interstate travelers or trucks; technology be used to collect tolls; and planning must consider the effects of diversion.

In encouraging PPPs more generally, the Commission suggests Congress require other criteria including a high level of transparency in the development of such agreements, full public participation, and full compliance with planning and environmental regulations. They also suggest that: PPP agreements should not contain non-compete clauses; toll rates should be capped; states should share in revenues over and above a certain set amount; concession agreements should not exceed a "reasonable" length; and an analysis be done to insure that private sector financing provides better value than public sector financing.

A minority of NSTPRSC commissioners issued a separate statement agreeing that Congress should encourage the use of PPPs, but argued that these new regulations would stifle their formation. As the minority statement in the report stated, the Commission proposes new Federal regulations of State contracts with the private sector. The Commission Report includes recommendations to replace what would otherwise be specifically negotiated terms and conditions with a national regulatory scheme for public-private partnerships that goes well beyond any regulations currently in place. In fact, despite finding substantial flaws with current programs and policies, the Commission Report strangely subjects innovative forms of project delivery to greater Federal scrutiny than traditional procurement approaches. The Commission Report would also subject private toll operators under contract with a State to greater Federal scrutiny than the scrutiny to which local public toll authorities are subject. There is no basis for this distinction.[85]

The Commission's minority view, therefore, suggests a third broad policy option for Congress to consider. This option would more aggressively encourage PPPs by providing program funding to encourage innovation and generally deregulating the use of tolling and private sector involvement, thereby letting states decide when and how to enter into agreements. This is also, in general terms, the position of the AASHTO officials. As they note in their policy report on revenue source in transportation:

> AASHTO has taken the position that every state should be given all options possible for funding opportunities in the areas of tolling and public — private ventures so states can determine for themselves what is in the best interests of their citizens. AASHTO has also embraced a bold goal of increasing the percentage of toll revenues to 9 percent of the total for highway revenues nationally. AASHTO's position is that federal policy should enable and encourage innovative finance tools and innovative contracting tools as well.[86]

The federal role in such a scenario may be mostly limited to providing guidance about instituting good practices and avoiding common pitfalls. Some past legislative proposals have linked deregulation in the area of tolling and public-private partnerships with devolution of federal responsibilities in highways and transit back to the states.[87]

Other policy options may arise from work being done by many different groups on surface transportation reauthorization proposals and recommendations. One of the most important is the National Surface Transportation Infrastructure Finance Commission (NSTIFC), a second national commission established in SAFETEA, charged with developing recommendations for Congress on the future federal role in funding surface transportation infrastructure. An interim report was released February 1, 2008,[88] and a final report is expected in 2009. Among other things, NSTIFC is expected to examine and make recommendations on the role that PPPs might play in the future.

In addition to policy decisions at the federal level, the future role of PPPs will also depend in large measure on decisions at the state and local level. States and localities rely on a wide variety of funding sources other than federal aid, including fuels taxes, other motor-vehicle taxes and fees, sales and property taxes, and general fund appropriations. The ability of states and localities to fund their systems with these revenue sources may determine how far and how fast PPPs are deployed. State and local innovation in PPPs, their successes and failures, and, ultimately, public acceptance also will be key determinants of deployment.

Federal influence on the prevalence and structure of PPPs, to some extent, will be related to the amount of federal funding flowing to state and local governments, an amount that is still largely dependent on the future financial health of the Highway Trust Fund. Declining inflation-adjusted revenues accruing to the trust fund, as a result of trends in fuel consumption and the level of prices in general, may result in a waning of federal influence on how highways and transit systems are built, maintained, and operated and the importance of PPPs. Declining inflation-adjusted revenues to the trust fund are not inevitable, however. The federal fuels tax is subject to change; it has been raised several times in the past. Alternatively, other federal funding mechanisms, such as national infrastructure bonds or even general fund appropriations, may emerge to fund a greater share of federal programs. Consequently, the federal role in shaping PPPs likely will be important for some time to come.

REFERENCES

[1] U.S. Department of Transportation, Federal Highway Administration, Public-Private Partnerships Website, "PPPs Defined." [http://www.fhwa. dot.gov/PPP/defined.htm].

[2]   Problems associated with estimating future infrastructure needs include defining a "need" and predicting future conditions, especially consumer demand which can vary depending on economic conditions and public policy choices such as how a service is funded and priced.

[3]   See, for example, Transportation Research Board, National Cooperative Highway Research Program, *Future Financing Options to Meet Highway and Transit Needs*, NCHRP Web- Only Document 102 (Washington, DC, 2006), p. 2-16. [http://onlinepubs.trb.org/onlinepubs/nchrp/nchrp_w 1 02.pdf].

[4]   U.S. Department of Transportation, Federal Highway Administration and Federal Transit Administration, *2006 Status of the Nation's Highways, Bridges, and Transit: Conditions and Performance* (Washington, DC, 2007). [http://www.fhwa.dot.gov/policy/2006cpr/index. htm].

[5]   National Surface Transportation Policy and Revenue Study Commission, *Transportation for Tomorrow* (Washington, DC, 2007). [http://www.transportation fortomorrow.org/final_ report/].

[6]   Ibid., Volume II, pages 4-6 and 4-12. High range estimates were 168% to 268% for highways and 78% to 162% for transit.

[7]   The federal tax on gasoline is currently 18.4 cents per gallon, of which 15.44 cents is deposited in the Highway Account of the Highway Trust Fund, 2.86 cents in the Mass Transit Account, and 0.1 cents in the Leaking Underground Storage Tank Trust Fund.

[8]   Estimates provided to CRS by the Congressional Budget Office, February 29, 2008.

[9]   U.S. Department of Labor, Bureau of Labor Statistics, Consumer Price Index.

[10] U.S. Department of Transportation, Federal Highway Administration, *Price Trends for Federal-Aid Highway Construction* (Washington, DC: 2008). [http://www.fhwa.dot.gov/ programadmin/pt2006q4.pdf].

[11] National Surface Transportation Policy and Revenue Study Commission, 2007, p. 60.

[12] U.S. Department of Transportation, Federal Highway Administration, Public Private Partnerships Website, "PPP Options." [http://www.fhwa.dot.gov/PPP/pcfs.htm].

[13] Government Accountability Office, *Highway Public-Private Partnerships: More Rigorous Up-front Analysis Could Better Secure Potential Benefits and Protect the Public Interest*, GAO-08-44 (Washington, DC, February 2008), p. 21. [http://www.gao.gov/

new.items/ 0844.pdf]; see also, "The Pros and Cons of Toll Road Leasing," Public Works Financing, Vol. 2005, May 2006, p. 1-11.

[14] Government Accountability Office, February 2008.

[15] Indiana Department of Transportation, Major Moves Website. [http://www.in.gov/indot/ 703 9.htm].

[16] Virginia Department of Transportation, Virginia Hot Lanes, "Capital Beltway Project Funding." [http://www.virginiahotlanes.com/ beltway-project-info-funding.asp].

[17] Fluor-Transurban, Virginia Hot Lanes Website. [http://www. virginiahot lanes.com/].

[18] McCabe, Francis, "Monorail Tax Break Renewed," *Las Vegas Review-Journal*, March 4, 2008, p. B2.

[19] General Accounting Office (now the Government Accountability Office), *Highways and Transit: Private Sector Sponsorship of Investment in Major Projects Has Been Limited*, GAO-04-419 (Washington, DC, March 2004), pp. 52-53. [http://www.gao.gov/new.items/ d04419.pdf].

[20] McCabe, Francis, "Monorail Extension Going Nowhere Fast," *Las Vegas Review-Journal*, January 13, 2008, p. B2.

[21] McCabe, Francis, March 4, 2008.

[22] McCabe, Francis, "Monorail Ridership Climbs in 2007," *Las Vegas Review-Journal*, January 19, 2008, p. B3.

[23] Missouri Department of Transportation, Safe and Sound Program Website. [http://www. modot.gov/safeandsound/index.htm].

[24] Ibid; see also Stokes, D.C., L. Gilroy, and S.R. Staley, "Missouri's Changing Transportation Paradigm," Show-Me Institute, *Policy Study*, No. 14, February 27, 2008. [http://showmeinstitute.org/docLib/ 20080225_smi_ study_14.pdf].

[25] U.S. Department of Transportation, Federal Highway Administration, "PPP Update: $3.37 Billion in Conditional Private Activity Bond Allocations Made," *Innovative Finance Quarterly*, Vol. 13, No. 2, Spring 2007. [http://www.fhwa.dot.gov/innovativeFinance/ ifqvol 1 3no2.htm].

[26] U.S. Department of Transportation, Federal Highway Administration and Federal Transit Administration, 2007, chapter 6.

[27] Ibid., exhibits 6-8 and 6-10.

[28] Ibid., exhibits 6-21 and 6-22.

[29] Perez, Benjamin G. and James W. March, "Public-Private Partnerships and the Development of Transport Infrastructure:

Trends on Both Side of the Atlantic," Paper Presented at the First Conference on Funding Transport Infrastructure, Banff, Alberta, Canada, August 2-3, 2006. [http://www.fhwa.dot.gov/PPP/ perez_banff_ppp_final.pdf].

[30] Ibid., p. 9.

[31] U.S. Department of Transportation, Federal Highway Administration, http://www.fhwa. dot.gov/PPP/legislation.htm].

[32] U.S. Department of Transportation, *Report to Congress on Public-Private Partnerships* (Washington, DC, 2004), p. 36. [http://www.fhwa.dot.gov/ reports/pppdec2004/pppdec2004. pdf].

[33] Transportation Research Board, Transit Cooperative Research Program, *Transit-Oriented Development in the United States: Experiences, Challenges, and Prospects*, TCRP Report 102 (Washington, DC, 2004). [http://onlinepubs.trb.org/ onlinepubs/tcrp/tcrp_rpt_102.pdf].

[34] At the outset, a number of existing toll roads were included as part of the Interstate Highway System.

[35] U.S. Department of Transportation, Federal Highway Administration, "Safe, Accountable, Flexible, Efficient Transportation Equity Act: A Legacy for Users (SAFETEA — LU); Opportunities for State and Other Qualifying Agencies To Gain Authority to Toll Facilities Constructed Using Federal Funds," 71 *Federal Register*, 965-969, January 6, 2006. [http://frwebgate. access.gpo.gov/cgi-bin/getpage.cgi?position=all and page=965 and dbname= 2006_register].

[36] U.S. Department of Transportation, Federal Highway Administration, Tolling and Pricing Website, "Value Pricing Pilot Program." [http://www.ops.fhwa. dot.gov/tolling_pricing/ value_pricing/index.htm].

[37] U.S. Department of Transportation, Federal Highway Administration, *Current Toll Road Activity in the U.S.: A Survey and Analysis* (Washington, DC, 2006). [http://www.fhwa. dot.gov/ppp/toll_survey_ 0906.pdf].

[38] U.S. Department of Transportation, Federal Highway Administration, *Innovative Finance Primer* (Washington, DC, 2002). [http://www.fhwa. dot.gov/innovativefinance/ifp/ifprimer. pdf].

[39] Hedlund, K.J. and N.C. Smith, "SAFETEA-LU Promotes Private Investment in Transportation," report prepared for Nossaman, Guther, Knox, and Elliott, LLP, August 1, 2005. [http://www.fhwa. dot.gov/PPP/safetea_lu_hedlund.pdf].

[40] CRS Report RL3 1457, *Private Activity Bonds: An Introduction*, by Steven Maguire.

[41] Testimony of JayEtta Hecker, Director, Physical Infrastructure Issues, General Accounting Office (now the Government Accountability Office), in U.S. Congress, Senate Committee on Finance and Committee on Environment and Public Works, September 25, 2002. [http://www.gao.gov/new.items/ d021 126t.pdf]; and Testimony of Peter Orzag, Director, Congressional Budget Office, in U.S. Congress, House Committee on the Budget and Committee on Transportation and Infrastructure, May 8, 2008. [http://www.cbo.gov/ftpdocs/91xx/doc9136/05-07-Infrastructure_Testimony. pdf].

[42] U.S. Congress, House Subcommittee on Highways and Transit, Hearing on Public-Private Partnerships: Innovative Contracting, "Summary of Subject Matter," April 12, 2007. [http://transportation.house.gov/Media/File/Highways/200704 17/SSM .pdf].

[43] Hedlund and Smith, 2005.

[44] U.S. Department of Transportation, 2004.

[45] U.S. Department of Transportation, Federal Transit Administration, *Innovative Financing Techniques for America's Transit Systems* (Washington, DC, 1998). [http://www.fta.dot. gov/planning/metro/planning_environment_3530.html].

[46] U.S. Department of Transportation, Federal Transit Administration, "Joint Development Guidance," 71 *Federal Register*, 5107-5109, January 31, 2006. [http://a257.g.akamaitech. net/7/257/2422/0 1j an2006 1 800/edocket. access. gpo.gov/2006/pdf/06-87 1 .pdf].

[47] U.S. Department of Transportation, Federal Transit Administration, "Notice of Final Agency Guidance on the Eligibility of Joint Development Improvements Under Federal Transit Law," 72 *Federal Register*, 5788-5800, February 7, 2007. [http://a257.g.akamaitech. net/7/257/2422/0 1j an2007 1 800/edocket.access.gpo.gov/2007/pdf/E7-1977.pdf].

[48] Samuel, Peter, "The Role of Tolls in Financing 21st Century Highways," Reason Foundation Policy Study 359, May 2007. [http://www. reason.org/ps359.pdf].

[49] Ibid., p. 29.

[50] Poole, Robert W. "Tolling and Public-Private Partnerships in Texas: Separating Myth from Fact," Reason Foundation Working Paper, May 2007.

[51] Ibid., p. 5.

[52] U.S. Department of Transportation, "Over $400 Billion Available Today for Road, Bridge and Transit Projects U.S. Secretary of Transportation Mary E. Peters Announces," Press Release, DOT 43-08, Wednesday, March 26, 2008.

[53] Orski, K., "A $400 Billion Solution," *Innovation Briefs*, Vol. 19, No. 8, March 10, 2008.

[54] Ibid.

[55] See McNally, Sean, "Investors Look to Banks for Help With Infrastructure Deals," *Transport Topics*, April 21, 2008, p. 14.

[56] To improve systems conditions and performance, DOT estimates annual increases in capital spending by as much as $61.4 billion for highways and $9.2 billion for transit.

[57] Transportation Research Board, 2006, p. 4-1; see also Organisation for Economic Cooperation and Development (OECD) and International Transport Forum, *Transport Infrastructure Investment: Options for Efficiency* (Paris, 2008); and General Accounting Office (now the Government Accountability Office), March 2004.

[58] Testimony of Pete Rahn, Director of the Missouri Department of Transportation and President of the American Association of State Highway and Transportation Officials (AASHTO), in U.S. Congress, House Committee on Transportation and Infrastructure, *Hearing on State Perspectives on Transportation for Tomorrow: Recommendations of the National Surface Transportation Policy and Revenue Study Commission*, February 13, 2008. [http://transportation.house. gov/Media/File /Highways/ 200802 1 3/Pete%20Rahn% 20Testimony. pdf].

[59] U.S. Department of Transportation, Federal Highway Administration and Federal Transit Administration, 2007, chapter 10.

[60] Steckler, Steve A. "Squeezing Cash from Concrete: Navigating the Perils of Turnpike Privatization." Infrastructure Management Group. [http://www.imggroup.com/transport ation/ documents/ Pennsylvania TollwayLeasing.pdf].

[61] Schmidt, John, "The Pros and Cons of Toll Road Leasing," *Public Works Financing*, Vol. 2005, May 2006, p. 9.

[62] Government Accountability Office, 2008, p. 21.

[63] Ibid., p. 34.

[64] Government Accountability Office, *Federal-Aid Highways: Trends, Effect on State Spending, and Options for Future Program Design*, GAO-04-802 (Washington, DC, 2004). [http://www.gao.gov/new.items/d04802.pdf].

[65] U.S. Department of Transportation, 2004, pp. 38-39.

[66] Testimony of Alan Lowenthal, Chair, California Senate Transportation and Housing Committee, in U.S. Congress, House Committee on Transportation and Infrastructure, Subcommittee on Highways and Transit, *Hearing on Public-Private Partnerships: State and User Perspectives*, May 24, 2007. [http://transportation.house.gov/Media/File/Highways/ 20070524/Cal%20State%20Senate%20Lowenthal %20testimony.pdf].

[67] Government Accountability Office, *Federal-Aid Highways: Increased Reliance on Contractors Can Pose Oversight Challenges for Federal and State Officials*, GAO-08-198 (Washington, DC, 2008). [http://www.gao.gov/new. items/d08 198.pdf].

[68] Engel, E., R. Fischer, and A. Galetovic, "Privatizing Highways in the United States," *Review of Industrial Organization*, 2006, Vol. 29.

[69] Government Accountability Office, 2008.

[70] U.S. Congress, House Subcommittee on Highways and Transit, *Hearing on Public-Private Partnerships: Innovative Financing and Protecting the Public Interest*, February 13, 2007. [http://www.house.gov/htbin/ leave_site? ln_url=http://frwebgate. access.gpo.gov/cgi-bin/getdoc.cgi?dbname= 110_ house_hearings and docid=f: 3477 8.pdf]; Government Accountability Office, 2008.

[71] Testimony of Gregory M. Cohen, President and CEO, American Highway Users Alliance, in U.S. Congress, House Subcommittee on Highways and Transit, *Hearing on Public- Private Partnerships: State and User Perspectives*, May 24, 2007. [http://transportation. house.gov/ Media/File/Highways/20070524/Greg%20Cohen%20Testimony.pdf].

[72] Testimony of Bill Graves, President and CEO of the American Trucking Associations, in U.S. Congress, House Subcommittee on Highways and Transit, *Public-Private Partnerships: State and User Perspectives*, May 24, 2007. [http://www.truckline.com/ NR/rdonlyres/5E923973-9F4D-46A3-A599-7 1F47FC7C3BE/0/PPPMay24_2007.pdf].

[73] Steckler; Cohen, 2007.

[74] Testimony of Tyler D. Duvall, Assistant Secretary of Transportation Policy, U.S. Department of Transportation, in U.S. Congress, House

Subcommittee on Highways and Transit, *Public-Private Partnerships: Financing and the Public Interest*, February 13, 2007. [http :// frwebgate.access .gpo.gov/cgi-bin/getdoc .cgi?dbname= 11 0_house_ hearings and docid=f:34778.pdf].

[75] Poole, May 2007.

[76] Swan, Peter F. and Michael H. Belzer, "Empirical Evidence of Toll Road Traffic Diversion and Implications for Highway Infrastructure Privatization," Paper presented at the 87th Annual Meeting of the Transportation Research Board, Washington, DC, January 2008.

[77] Ibid.

[78] U.S. Department of Transportation, "Low-Income Equity Concerns of U.S. Road Pricing Initiatives." [http://www.upa.dot.gov/resources/ lwincequityrpi/ index.htm].

[79] Testimony of R. Syms, County Executive of King County, Washington, in U.S. Congress, House Subcommittee on Highways and Transit, *Hearing on Transportation Challenges of Metropolitan Areas*, April 9, 2008.

[80] Edward Hill et al., "Slanted Pavement: How Ohio's Highway Spending Shortchanges Cities and Suburbs," in Bruce Katz and Robert Puentes, eds., *Taking the High Road: A Metropolitan Agenda for Transportation Reform* (Washington, DC: Brookings Institution Press, 2005); U.S. General Accounting Office (now the Government Accountability Office), *Surface Transportation: Many Factors Affect Investment Decisions*, GAO-04-744 (Washington, DC, June 2004), at [http://www.gao.gov/new. items/d04744.pdf].

[81] Testimony of John Foote, in U.S. Congress, House Subcommittee on Highways, Transit, and Pipelines, *Hearing on Understanding Contemporary Public Private Highway Transactions — the Future of Infrastructure Finance*, May 24, 2006.

[82] Poole, May 2007, p. 8.

[83] Ibid.; See also "The Chicago Skyway Sale," *Public Works Financing*, Vol. 205, May 2006, p. 4-11.

[84] Government Accountability Office, 2008; see also Buxbaum, Jeffrey N. and Iris N. Oritz, "Protecting the Public Interest: The Role of Long-Term Concession Agreements for Providing Transportation Infrastructure," USC Keston Institute for Public Finance and Infrastructure Policy, Research Paper 07-02, June 2007.

[85] National Surface Transportation Policy and Revenue Study Commission, 2007, p. 66.

[86] Association of State Highway and Transportation Officials, *Revenue Sources to Fund Transportation Needs* (Washington, DC, September 2007), p. 12. [http://www.transportation 1.org/tif4report/TIF4-1.pdf].

[87] Utt, Ronald D. "Proposal to Turn the Federal Highway Program Back to States Would Relieve Traffic Congestion," *Heritage Foundation Backg rounder*, No. 1709, November 21, 2003. [http://www.heritage.org/ Research/SmartGrowth/upload/5277 1_1 .pdf].

[88] National Surface Transportation Infrastructure Finance Commission, *The Path Forward: Funding and Financing Our Surface Transportation System* (Washington, DC, 2008). [http://financecommission.dot. gov/Documents/Interim%20Report%20-%20The%20Path%0Forward.pdf].

In: Public-Private Partnerships   ISBN: 978-1-60692-358-0
Editor: Leslie R. Kellerman, pp. 39-129   © 2009 Nova Science Publishers, Inc.

Chapter 2

HIGHWAY PUBLIC-PRIVATE PARTNERSHIPS. MORE RIGOROUS UP-FRONT ANALYSIS COULD BETTER SECURE POTENTIAL BENEFITS AND PROTECT THE PUBLIC INTEREST[*]

U.S. Government Accountability Office

ABBREVIATIONS

CDA	comprehensive development agreement
CPI	consumer price index
DOT	Department of Transportation
ETR	Express Toll Road
FHWA	Federal Highway Administration
GDP	gross domestic product
ISTEA	Intermodal Surface Transportation Efficiency Act of 1991
ITRCC	Indiana Toll Road Concession Company
LOS	level of service
NEPA	National Environmental Policy Act
OMB	Office of Management and Budget
OTIG	Oregon Transportation Improvement Group

PAB	private activity bond
PSC	public sector comparator
RFP	request for proposals
SAFETEA-LU	Safe, Accountable, Flexible, Efficient Transportation Equity Act—A Legacy for Users
SCC	Skyway Concession Company
SEP	Special Experimental Project
SR	State Road
TEA-21	Transportation Equity Act for the 21st Century
TIFIA	Transportation Infrastructure Finance and Innovation Act of 1998
TE-045	Innovative Finance Test and Evaluation Program
TTC	Trans-Texas Corridor
U.S.C.	United States Code
VfM	Value for Money

February 8, 2008
Congressional Requesters

America's transportation system is the essential element that facilitates the movement of both people and freight within the country. Both economic activity and mobility are dependent upon an efficient transportation system. The United States is at a critical juncture regarding its ability to address demands on the transportation system. The Safe, Accountable, Flexible, Efficient Transportation Equity Act—A Legacy for Users (SAFETEA-LU) authorized about $286 billion for highway, transit, and other transportation system spending for the 6-year period ending in fiscal year 2009. However, the Highway Trust Fund, the principal mechanism for providing federal funds for highway programs, could have a negative balance as early as 2012.[1] More specifically, under current law, the Highway Account, which makes up the majority of Highway Trust Fund receipts, is projected to have a negative balance by 2009 due to a growing difference between projected receipts—the federal excise tax on motor fuel and truck-related taxes are primary sources of revenue for the Highway Account—and outlays. Baring changes to the tax structure, the situation will likely be further exacerbated by inflation and more fuel efficient vehicles that will act to further erode the resources available to meet transportation system demands. In 2005, the

---

[*] Excerpted from GAO Report GAO-08-44, dated February 2008.

federal government accounted for about 40 percent of highway program capital spending (see figure 1). State and local governments accounted for about 60 percent of highway program capital spending.

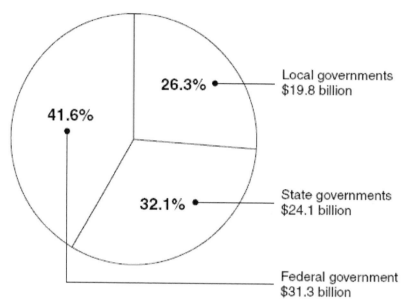

Source: Federal Highway Administration.

Figure 1. Total Capital Spending on Highways, by Level of Government, Fiscal Year 2005.

The nation is also on an imprudent and unsustainable fiscal path. As the baby-boomer generation retires, entitlement programs will grow and require increasing shares of federal spending in the years ahead. Absent significant changes to tax and spending programs and policies, we face a future of unsustainable deficits and debt that threatens to cripple our economy and quality of life. This looming fiscal crisis requires a fundamental reexamination of all government programs and commitments by reviewing their results and testing their continued relevance and relative priority in the twenty-first century. This reexamination offers the prospect of addressing emerging needs (1) by weeding out programs and policies that are outdated or ineffective and (2) by modernizing those programs and policies that remain relevant. The federal programs for highways are particularly ripe for reexamination. The Interstate Highway System has been completed, yet the basic structure of the federal-aid highway program has not changed. As we have reported, federal transportation programs do not have mechanisms to link funding levels with the accomplishment of specific performance-related goals and outcomes related to mobility, and most highway grant programs are apportioned by formula, without regard to the needs or capacity of recipients.[2] Transportation and other experts on a panel recently convened by the Comptroller General stated that the nation's transportation policy has lost focus and that the nation's overall transportation goals need to be better defined and linked to performance measures that evaluate what the respective policies and programs actually accomplish.[3] There was broad consensus among the participants on the need for a transformation of our current approach to transportation policy to better meet current and future mobility needs in a strategic, integrated, and sustainable manner.

Finally, the nation faces increasing congestion on the nation's highways. According to a February 2007 American Association of State Highway and Transportation Officials report, Federal Highway Administration (FHWA) has forecasted that over the next 50 years highway vehicle miles of travel will more than double from 3 trillion to 7 trillion.[4] To meet the growing demand for new transportation capacity, states and localities are looking for alternatives to direct government provision of transportation infrastructure and services. One of these alternatives is increased private sector participation in delivering the infrastructure and services that the public sector is struggling to keep up with.

The private sector has traditionally been involved as contractors in the design and construction of highways. In recent years, the private sector has become increasingly involved in assuming other responsibilities including planning, designing, and financing. The private sector has also entered into a wide variety of highway public-private partnership arrangements with public agencies. According to FHWA, the term "public-private-partnership" is used for any scenario under which the private sector assumes a greater role in the planning, financing, design, construction, operation, and maintenance of a transportation facility compared to traditional procurement methods.[5] Under some of these alternative arrangements, the private sector is increasingly being looked at to not only construct facilities but also to finance, maintain, and operate such infrastructure under long-term leaseholds—up to 99 years in some cases. In some cases, this involves financing and constructing a new facility and then operating and maintaining it over a specified period of time, while in other cases it involves operating and maintaining an existing toll road for a period of time in exchange for an up-front payment provided to the public sector. Proponents of these forms of highway public-private partnerships contend that they offer the potential advantages of obtaining critical new or expanded infrastructure sooner than if provided solely by the public sector, at a potentially lower cost given the efficiencies and innovation of market-driven private companies, and the use of private rather than public funds. In addition, risks of major infrastructure projects, such as risks associated with constructing highways and risks of generating sufficient traffic and revenue for financial viability, can be shifted from the public to the private sector. Since these arrangements are often used in relation to toll roads, the private sector return is achieved through the collection of future toll revenue. However, highway public-private partnership arrangements are not "risk free," and concerns have been raised about how well the public interest has been evaluated and protected. Concerns have also been raised about the potential loss of public control over critical assets for up to 99 years.

In January 2008, the National Surface Transportation Policy and Revenue Study Commission issued its report on the surface transportation system.[6] The commission was required, among other things, to conduct a comprehensive study of the current condition and future needs of the surface transportation system and develop a conceptual plan, with alternative approaches, to ensure that the surface transportation system continues to serve the needs of the United States. The report made a number of recommendations for restructuring and financing the nation's surface transportation programs, in order to align federal leadership and federal transportation investments with national interests in the areas of highways, transit, passenger rail, freight, and other areas. The report also contained recommendations on tolling, congestion pricing, and the use of public-private partnerships. These recommendations included providing states and localities the flexibility to use tolls to fund new capacity on the Interstate Highway System and the flexibility to implement congestion pricing on this system—on both new and existing capacity in metropolitan areas with populations greater than 1 million. The report encouraged the use of public-private partnerships, including concessions, for highways and other surface transportation modes, and stated that "public-private partnerships should play an important role in financing and managing our surface transportation system." The commission recommended criteria to be included in public-private partnership concessions, including requirements that states cap toll rates (at the level of the consumer price index (CPI) minus a productivity adjustment), prohibit the use of revenues for nontransportation purposes, avoid toll rates that discriminate against certain users, and fully consider the effect tolling might have on diverting traffic to other facilities. The commission also recommended that there be increased transparency and adequate public participation in the decision to use public-private partnerships, revenue sharing between states and private concessionaires, and a demonstration that private sector financing provides better value for money than if the concession were financed using public funds.

To assist Congress as it assesses the future of federal surface transportation and highway programs, you asked us to identify the issues associated with increased use of private sector participation in providing transportation infrastructure to the public. In response to your request, this chapter addresses (1) the benefits, costs, and trade-offs associated with highway public-private partnerships; (2) how public officials have identified and acted to protect the public interest in highway public-private partnership arrangements; and (3) the federal role in highway public-private partnerships and potential changes in this role.

For purposes of this chapter, we limited the term "highway public-private partnerships" to highway-related projects in which the public sector enters into a contract, lease, or concession agreement with a private sector firm or firms, and where the private sector provides transportation services such as designing, constructing, operating, and maintaining the facility, usually for an extended period of time. This definition included long-term concessions for toll roads in which the private sector firm(s) receives some or all toll revenues over the life of the lease or concession agreement with the public sector. There are numerous other types of arrangements which the Department of Transportation (DOT) classifies as "public-private partnerships" that we did not include. For example, we did not include fee-for-service arrangements in which effective ownership of a transportation facility does not transfer to the private sector, nor did we include arrangements where concessionaires are only paid for services provided or public-private partnerships that might be used to allow the private sector to improve federal real property. This chapter is focused on the use of public-private partnerships in highways, although we recognize that such public-private partnerships can be used to provide other transportation (e.g., transit) and outside the transportation sector, such as hospitals and prisons. We also recognize that there may be other forms of highway public-private partnerships, such as shadow tolling in which the public sector pays a private sector company an amount per user of a roadway and there is no direct collection of a toll by the private company, or availability payments in which a private company is paid based on the availability of a highway to users. We did not include any of these types of public-private partnerships in the scope of our chapter, and the findings and conclusions of this chapter cannot be extrapolated to those or other types of public-private partnerships.

To address these issues, we reviewed pertinent federal legislation and regulations, including SAFETEA-LU, as well as federal guidance and relevant modifications of FHWA procedures to permit the use of highway public-private partnerships on federally supported projects. We also collected data and analyzed information related to one project in Canada—the 407 Express Toll Road (ETR) near Toronto—and four projects in the United States—two were leases of existing transportation facilities and two were new construction projects—where such highway public-private partnerships had been, or were expected to be, used: (1) Chicago Skyway, Chicago, Illinois; (2) Indiana Toll Road, Indiana; (3) projects in and around the Portland, Oregon, area; and (4) the Trans-Texas Corridor (TTC), Texas. This included obtaining descriptions of these projects, copies of the concession or development agreements, and documentation related to the financial structure of such projects. These projects were selected because they were recent examples of highway public-private partnerships, were large dollar projects, or used different approaches. We also interviewed other states that were considering highway public-private partnerships for their highways, including California, New Jersey, and Pennsylvania. Our work also collected data and information on the use of highway public-private partnerships in Australia, Canada, and Spain. Further, we collected information on how public interest is evaluated in privately financed initiatives in the United Kingdom. All of these countries are leaders in using highway public-private partnerships to obtain transportation infrastructure. Finally, we interviewed FHWA and other federal officials, state and local officials associated with the three projects we selected, and with private sector officials involved with U.S. highway public-private partnership arrangements. We also conducted extensive interviews with government and private sector officials in Australia, Canada, and Spain. (See app. I for a more detailed discussion of our scope and methodology.)

We conducted this performance audit from June 2006 to February 2008 in accordance with generally accepted government auditing standards. Those standards require that we plan and perform the audit to obtain sufficient, appropriate evidence to provide a reasonable basis for our findings and conclusions based on our audit objectives. We believe that the evidence obtained provides a reasonable basis for our findings and conclusions based on our audit objectives.

RESULTS IN BRIEF

Highway public-private partnerships have the potential to provide numerous benefits to the public sector as well as potential costs and trade-offs. Highway public-private partnerships created to date have resulted in advantages from the perspective of state and local governments, such as the construction of new infrastructure without using public funding and obtaining funds by extracting value from existing facilities for reinvestment in transportation and other public programs. For example, the state of Indiana received $3.8 billion from leasing the Indiana Toll Road and used those proceeds to fund a 10-year statewide transportation plan. Highway public-private partnerships potentially provide other benefits, including the transfer or sharing of project risks to the private sector. Such risks include those associated with construction costs and schedules and having sufficient levels of traffic and revenues to be financially viable. In addition, the public sector can potentially benefit from increased efficiencies in operations and life-cycle management, such as increased use of innovative technologies. Finally, through the use of tolling, highway public-private partnerships offer the potential to price highways to better reflect the true costs of operating and maintaining them and to increase mobility by adjusting tolls to manage demand, as well as the potential for more cost effective investment decisions by private investors. There are also potential costs and trade-offs to highway public-private partnerships. There is no "free" money—while highway public-private partnerships can be used to obtain financing for highway infrastructure without the use of public sector funding, this funding is a form of privately issued debt that must be repaid to private investors seeking a return on their investment by collecting toll revenues. Though concession agreements can limit the extent to which a concessionaire can raise tolls, it is likely that tolls will increase on a privately operated highway to a greater extent than they would on a publicly operated toll road. To the extent that a private concessionaire gains market power by control of a road where there are not other viable travel alternatives that would not require substantially more travel time, the potential also exists that the public could pay tolls that are higher than tolls based on cost of the facilities, including a reasonable rate of return. Furthermore, by leasing existing facilities, the public sector may give up more than it gains if the net present value of the future stream of revenues (less operating and capital costs) given up exceeds the concession payment received. Conversely, because the private sector takes on potentially substantial risks, the opposite could also be true—that is, the public sector might gain more than it gives up. Additionally, because large up-front concession payments have in part been used to fund immediate needs, it remains to be seen whether these agreements will provide long-term benefits to future generations who will potentially be paying progressively higher toll rates throughout the length of a concession agreement. Highway public-private partnerships also potentially require additional costs compared with traditional public procurement—for example, the costs associated with the need to hire financial and legal advisors. Further, while risks can be shared in highway public-private partnerships, not all risks can or should be shared, such as environmental or political risks. Finally, as with any highway project, there are multiple stakeholders and potential objectives and trade-offs in protecting the public interest.

Public officials in the highway public-private partnership projects that we reviewed identified and protected the public interest, largely through terms contained in concession contracts, and in the United States we found more limited use of more formal tools such as those used in some other countries to evaluate and protect the public interest. Most often the terms of the contract focused on ensuring the performance of the facility (e.g., requirements for maintenance and expansion) and dealing with issues such as toll rates, public sector flexibility to provide future transportation services to the public, and workforce issues. Furthermore, the terms contained oversight and monitoring mechanisms to ensure that private partners fulfilled their obligations. Financial analyses, such as public sector comparators (PSC) that can be used to compare the costs of a proposed highway public-private partnership project with expected costs of procuring the project publicly, have also been used by some projects in the United States. Governments in other countries, including Australia and the United Kingdom have developed systematic approaches to identifying and evaluating public interest before agreements are entered into, including the use of public interest criteria, as well as assessment tools, and require their use when considering private investments in public infrastructure. For example, a state government in Australia uses a public interest test to determine how the public interest would be affected in eight specific areas, including whether the views and rights of affected communities have been heard and protected and whether the process is sufficiently transparent. While similar tools have been used to some extent in the United States, their use has been more limited. Not using such tools may lead to certain aspects of protecting public interest being overlooked. For example, concerns by local and regional governments in Texas resulted in statewide legislation requiring the state to involve local and regional governments to a greater extent in future highway public-private partnerships. Elsewhere, in Toronto, Canada, the lack of a transparency about the toll rate structure and misunderstanding about the toll structure of the 407 ETR facility was a major factor in significant opposition to the project. Using up-front public interest analysis tools can also assist public agencies in determining the expected benefits and costs of a project and an appropriate means to undergo the project.

Direct federal involvement in highway public-private partnerships has generally been limited to projects in which federal requirements must be followed because federal funds have or will be used. While direct federal involvement has been limited to date in the highway public-private partnerships we reviewed, the administration and the DOT have actively promoted highway public-private partnerships through policies and practices, including the development of experimental programs that waive certain federal regulations and encourage private investment. Recent highway public-private partnerships have involved sizable investments of funds and significant facilities and could pose national public interest implications such as interstate commerce that may transcend whether there is direct federal investment in a project. For example, although the Indiana Toll Road is part of the Interstate Highway System, minimal federal funds were used to construct it, and those funds were repaid to the federal government. Thus, although over 60 percent of the traffic on the road (according to one study) is interstate in nature, federal officials had little involvement in reviewing the terms of this concession agreement, and FHWA did not review any potential impacts on interstate commerce—or require the state of Indiana to review these issues—before it was signed. Texas envisions constructing new international border crossings and freight corridors as part of the TTC, which may greatly facilitate North American Free Trade Agreement-related truck traffic to other states. However, no federal funding has been expended in the development of the project to date. Given the minimal federal funding in highway public-private partnerships to date, few mechanisms exist to consider potential national public interests in them. For example, FHWA officials told us that no federal definition of public interest or federal guidance on identifying and evaluating public interest exists. The absence of a clear identification and furtherance of national public interests in the national transportation system is not unique to highway public-private partnerships. We have called for a fundamental reexamination of the federal role in highways, including a clear identification of specific national interests in the system.

Such a reexamination would provide an opportunity to establish the national public interest in highway public-private partnerships and form the basis for how this interest can best be furthered. We also found that highway public-private partnerships that have or will use federal funds and involve tolling may be required by law to use excess toll revenues (revenues that are beyond that needed for debt service, a reasonable return on investment to a private party, and operation and maintenance of a toll facility) for projects eligible for federal transportation funding. However, the methodology for calculating excess toll revenues is not clear.

To ensure that future highway public-private partnerships meet federal requirements concerning the use of excess revenues for federally eligible transportation purposes, we recommend that the Secretary of Transportation direct the Federal Highway Administrator to clarify federal-aid highway regulations on the methodology for determining excess toll revenue, including a reasonable rate of return to private investors in highway public-private partnerships that involve federal investment. In order to balance the potential benefits of highway public-private partnerships with protecting public and national interests, Congress should consider directing the Secretary of Transportation, in consultation with Congress and other stakeholders, to develop and submit to Congress objective criteria for identifying national public interests in highway public-private partnerships. In developing these criteria, the Secretary should identify any additional legal authority, guidance, or assessment tools required, as appropriate and needed, to ensure national public interests are protected in future highway public-private partnerships. The criteria should be crafted to allow the department to play a targeted role in ensuring that national interests are considered in highway public-private partnerships, as appropriate.

We provided copies of the draft chapter to the Department of Transportation for comment. The Assistant Secretary for Transportation Policy and the Deputy Assistant Secretary for Transportation Policy provided comments in a meeting with us on November 30, 2007. DOT raised substantive concerns and disagreed with several of the draft chapter's findings and conclusions, as well as one recommendation. We clarified the chapter and made other changes, as appropriate. For example, we revised the chapter to better clarify the potential benefits of pricing and resource efficiencies of highway public-private partnerships that DOT cited in its comments and added information about initiatives that certain states have taken to identify and protect the public interest in highway public-private partnerships. We recommended that the Secretary of Transportation direct the Administrator of FHWA to clarify federal-aid highway regulations on the methodology for determining excess toll revenue, including a reasonable rate of return to private investors in highway public-private partnerships. DOT said it would reexamine the regulations and take appropriate action, as necessary, to ensure the regulations are clear. Therefore, we made no change to the recommendation. Our draft chapter also recommended that DOT develop a legislative proposal containing objective criteria for identifying the national public interests in highway public-private partnerships. DOT disagreed with this recommendation, stating it would involve intrusion by the federal government into inherently state activities and a more expansive federal role. We believe the reexamination of federal transportation programs, which we have previously called for, provides an opportunity to identify national interests in the transportation system and determine the most appropriate federal role. Once established, we believe the federal government can play a more targeted, not necessarily more expansive, role. We have, therefore, deleted our recommendation and instead are suggesting that Congress consider directing DOT to undertake this action. DOT and other agencies (including state and foreign governments we spoke with) also provided technical. comments that were incorporated, as appropriate. DOT's comments and our evaluation are discussed at the end of this chapter.

BACKGROUND

Private sector participation and investment in highways is not new. In the 1800s, private companies built many roads that were financed with revenues from tolls, but this activity declined due to competition from railroads and greater state and federal involvement in building tax-supported highways. Private sector involvement in highways was relegated to contracting with states to build roads. In the absence of private toll roads, states and local governments were responsible for road construction and maintenance. In the 1930s many states began creating public authorities that built toll roads such as the Pennsylvania Turnpike that relied on loans and private investors buying bonds to finance construction. The Federal-Aid Highway Act of 1956 established a federal tax-assisted National System of Interstate and Defense Highways, commonly know as the Interstate Highway System. Further, the federal Highway Revenue Act of 1956 established a Highway Trust Fund to be funded using revenue from, among other sources, motor fuel taxes. The Federal-Aid Highway Act of 1956 generally prohibited the use of federal funds for the construction, reconstruction, or improvement of any toll road.

States retain the primary responsibility for building and maintaining highways. While states collect revenues to finance road construction and maintenance from a variety of sources, including fuel taxes, they also receive significant federal funding. For example, in 2005, of the $75.2 billion spent on highways by all levels of government, about $31.3 billion (about 42 percent) was federal funding. Federal highway funding is distributed mostly through a series of formula grant programs, collectively known as the federal-aid highway program. Funding for the federal-aid highway program is provided through the Highway Trust Fund—a fund that was used to finance construction of the Interstate Highway System on a "pay as you go" basis. Receipts for the Highway Trust Fund are derived from two main sources: federal excise taxes on motor fuel and truck-related taxes. Receipts from federal excise taxes on motor fuel constitute the single largest source of revenue for the Highway Account. Funds are provided to the states for capital projects, such as new construction, reconstruction, and many forms of capital-intensive maintenance. These funds are available for eligible projects and pay 80 percent of the costs on most projects. Additionally, the responsibility for planning and selecting projects is handled by the states and metropolitan planning organizations.

Over time, federal programs and legislation have gradually become more receptive to private sector participation and investment. For example, the Surface Transportation and Uniform Relocation Assistance Act of 1987 established a pilot program allowing federal participation in financing the construction or reconstruction of seven toll facilities, excluding highways on the Interstate Highway System. Construction costs for these projects were eligible for a 35 percent federal-aid match. The Intermodal Surface Transportation Efficiency Act of 1991 (ISTEA) removed the pilot project limitation on federal participation in financing the initial construction or reconstruction of tolled facilities, including the conversion of nontolled to tolled facilities. ISTEA raised the federal share of construction costs on toll roads to 50 percent and allowed federal participation in financing privately owned and operated toll roads, provided that the public authority remained responsible for ensuring that all of its title 23 responsibilities to the federal government were met. ISTEA also included a congestion pricing pilot program that allowed the Secretary of Transportation to enter into cooperative agreements with up to five state or local governments or public authorities to establish, maintain, and monitor congestion pricing projects.

In 1998, the Transportation Equity Act for the 21st Century (TEA-21) renamed the congestion pricing pilot, calling it a "value-pricing pilot program," and expanded the number of projects eligible for assistance to 15. TEA-21 also created a pilot program for tolling roads in the Interstate Highway System. Under this pilot, up to three states can toll interstates if the purpose is to reconstruct or rehabilitate the road and the state could not adequately maintain or improve the road without collecting tolls. Finally, the Transportation Infrastructure Finance and Innovation Act of 1998 (TIFIA) created a new federal program to assist in the financing of major transportation projects, in part by encouraging private sector investment in infrastructure. The TIFIA program permits the Secretary of Transportation to offer secured loans, loan guarantees, and lines of credit.

In 2005, SAFETEA-LU reauthorized appropriations to fund all of the previously established toll programs. SAFETEA-LU also allowed the combining of public and private sector funds, including the investment of public funds in private sector facility improvements for purposes of eligibility for TIFIA loans. SAFETEA-LU also created the Express Lanes Demonstration Program, which authorizes the Secretary of Transportation to fund 15 demonstration projects to use tolling of highways, bridges, or tunnels—including facilities on the Interstate

Highway System—to manage high congestion levels, reduce emissions in nonattainment or maintenance areas under the Clean Air Act, or finance highway expansion to reduce congestion. Finally, SAFETEA-LU amended the Internal Revenue Code to add qualified highway or surface freight transfer facilities to the types of privately developed and operated projects for which exempt facility bonds (also called private activity bonds, PABs) may be issued.[7] According to FHWA, passage of the PAB provisions reflected the federal government's desire to increase private sector investment in U.S. transportation infrastructure. SAFETEA-LU authorized the Secretary of Transportation to allocate up to $15 billion in PABs for qualifying highway and freight transfer facilities. As of January 2008, about $3.2 billion in PABs had been approved by DOT.

The private sector has historically been involved in the construction phase as a contractor. Over time, the private sector has been increasingly involved in other phases of projects serving as either contractors or managers (see figure 2). The private sector has become more involved in a wide range of tasks, including design, planning, preliminary engineering, and maintenance of highways. In addition, contractors have been given more responsibility for project oversight and ensuring project quality through increased use of contractors for engineering and inspection activities, as well as quality assurance activities. This increasing use of contractors can, in part, be attributed to the need for staff and expertise by state highway agencies. Existing surveys of state highway departments from 1996 to 2002 show an increase of tasks completely outsourced from about 26 percent to about 36 percent.[8]

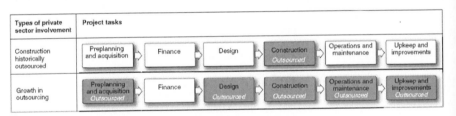

Source: GAO.
Note: Dark shading indicates private sector involvement.

Figure 2. Evolution of Private Sector Involvement with Highway Projects.

Private sector participation can also involve highway public-private partnerships. As highway public-private partnerships can be defined to include any private sector involvement beyond the traditional contracting role in construction, there are many types of highway public-private partnership models. For example, design-build contracts, in which a private partner both designs and then constructs a highway under a single contract, is considered by DOT to be a highway public-private partnership. Some highway public-private partnerships involve equity investments by the private sector (see figure 3). In construction of new infrastructure, commonly called "greenfield projects," the private sector may provide financing for construction of the facility and then has responsibility for all operations and maintenance of the highway for a specified amount of time. The private operator generally makes its money through the collection of tolls. Private investments have also been made in existing infrastructure through the long-term leases of currently existing toll roads. These transactions, often called "brownfield" projects, usually involve a private operator assuming control of the asset—including responsibilities for maintenance and operation and collection of toll revenues—for a fixed period of time in exchange for a concession fee provided to the public sector. The concession fee could be in the form of an up-front payment at the start of the concession, or could be provided over time through a revenue sharing arrangement, or both. While many long-term public-private partnerships involve tolled highways, that is not necessarily always the case. For example, under a "shadow tolling" arrangement, the private sector finances, constructs, and operates a nontolled highway for a period of time and is paid a predetermined fee per car by the public sector.

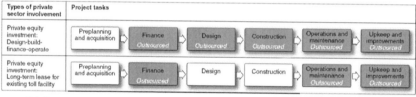

Source: GAO.
Note: Dark shading indicates private sector involvement.

Figure 3. Private Equity Investments in Highway Public-Private Partnerships.

The projects included as part of our review primarily involved the long-term concessions of toll roads involving private sector equity. This model has seen strong interest in the past few years as many states have considered using this model to construct new highway infrastructure. For example, Texas is currently developing a number of new highways through this model. In addition, many states have explored private involvement for the long-term operation and maintenance of existing toll roads. For example, the city of Chicago and the state of Indiana recently entered into long-term leases with the private sector for the Chicago Skyway and Indiana Toll Road, respectively. Since we began our review, other states have begun exploring leasing existing toll roads to the private sector. For example, Pennsylvania has considered many options, including a long-term lease, for extracting value from the Pennsylvania Turnpike. In 2006, Virginia entered into a long-term lease agreement with a private company for the Pocahontas Parkway in the Richmond area and, in 2007, the Northwest Parkway Public Highway Authority entered into a long-term concession in the Denver region.

The U.S. highway public-private partnership projects included in our review were varied (see table 1). Two of the projects—the TTC and Oregon—involved construction of infrastructure. The Texas project, in particular, was envisioned as an extensive network of interconnected corridors that involved passenger and freight movement, as well as passenger and freight railroads. The Oregon projects were primarily in the Portland area and involved capacity enhancement. Two of the projects we reviewed also involved leases of existing facilities—the Indiana Toll Road and the Chicago Skyway. In both instances, local or state officials were looking to extract value from the assets for reinvestment in transportation or other purposes. (See app. II for more information about the highway public-private partnerships that were included in our review.)

Table 1. Description of U.S. Highway Public-Private Partnerships Reviewed by GAO

Name and location	Description	Date leased or project initiated
New construction		
TTC, Texas	The TTC is envisioned in total to be a 4,000 mile statewide network of interconnected corridors containing tolled highways and separate tolled truckways, as well as freight, intercity, and commuter rail lines and possible utility easements. In June 2002, the Texas Transportation Commission adopted an action plan identifying priority segments of the TTC. In 2005, the Texas DOT awarded a comprehensive development agreement to a private consortium to develop preliminary concept and financing plans for the first portion of the TTC (TTC-35) from Oklahoma to Mexico. This agreement also allows the concessionaire to bid on other projects known as "connecting facilities." In 2007, the Texas DOT also awarded a 50-year concession to the private consortium to develop State Highway 130, segments 5 and 6. This is expected to be a connecting facility to the TTC. State Highway 130 is a new highway being built in segments between Austin and San Antonio in central Texas.	June 2002

Table 1. (Continued).

Name and location*	Description	Date leased or project initiated
Oregon	In January 2006, the Oregon Transportation Commission approved agreements with the Oregon Transportation Improvement Group (a private sector partner) for predevelopment work on three proposed projects—construction of roads east of Portland (Sunrise Corridor), South I-205 widening, and construction of an 11-mile highway in the Newberg-Dundee area.	January 2006
Lease of existing facilities		
Chicago Skyway, Chicago, Illinois	The Chicago Skyway was originally built in 1958 and was operated and maintained by the city of Chicago Department of Streets and Sanitation. It is a 7.8 mile elevated toll road connecting I-94 (Dan Ryan Expressway) in Chicago to I-90 (Indiana Toll Road) at the Indiana border. In October 2004, it was leased to a private concessionaire under a 99-year lease for about $1.8 billion.	October 2004
Indiana Toll Road, Indiana	The Indiana Toll Road has been operational since 1956 and stretches 157 miles along the northern most border of Indiana. From 1981 to 2006, it was operated by Indiana DOT. Since June 2006, it has been operated by a private concessionaire under a 75-year lease. Indiana received $3.8 billion from the lease.	June 2006

Source: GAO analysis of project data.

There has been considerable private participation in highways and other infrastructure internationally. Europe, in particular has been a leader in use of these arrangements. Spain and France pioneered the use of highway public-private partnerships for the development of tolled motorways in Europe. Spain began inviting concessionaires to build a national *autopista* network in the 1960s, while private *autoroute* concessions in France date from the 1970s. Public-private partnership arrangements for infrastructure project financing or delivery of highway-related projects is widespread among the regions of the world.[9] Highway public-private partnership initiatives support continued economic growth in more developed parts of the world or foster economic development in the less developed parts of the world. Over the period 1985 to 2004, the highest investment in road projects (includes roads, bridges, and tunnels) funded and completed using public-private partnerships was in Europe ($58.1 billion) followed by Asia ($44.5 billion) and North America ($32.2 billion). (See figure 4.) FHWA attributed the predominant role of Europe to the absence of a dedicated funding source for highways and a rapid transition in the 1990s from a largely public infrastructure system to a more privately financed, developed, and operated system, among other things.

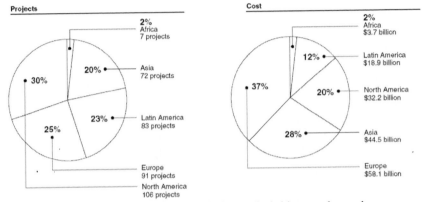

Note: The term "highway infrastructure" includes roads, bridges, and tunnels.
Source: FHWA..

Figure 4. Worldwide Highway Infrastructure Projects Funded and Completed Using Public-Private Partnerships, 1985 to October 2004, by Region.

HIGHWAY PUBLIC-PRIVATE PARTNERSHIPS CAN POTENTIALLY PROVIDE BENEFITS BUT ALSO ENTAIL COSTS, RISKS, AND TRADE-OFFS

While highway public-private partnerships have the potential to provide numerous benefits, they also entail costs and trade-offs to the public sector. The advantages and potential benefits of highway public-private partnerships, as well as their costs and trade-offs are summarized in table 2. Highway public-private partnerships that involve tolling may not be suited to all situations. In addition to potential benefits to the public sector, highway public-private partnerships can potentially provide private sector benefits as well through investment in a long-term asset with steady income generation over the course of a concession and availability of various tax incentives.

Table 2. Potential Benefits, Costs, and Trade-offs Associated with Highway Public-Private Partnerships

Advantages and potential benefits for the public sector	Potential costs/trade-offs for the public sector
Finance the construction of new highways without the use of public funding.	Tolls paid by road users, regardless of whether the collector is in the private sector or the public sector. Potentially higher tolls under private operation.
Obtain up-front payments through the long-term lease of existing toll roads.	Public may give up more than it gains if tolls over time exceed the value of up-front payments. Use of proceeds for short-term compared with long-term uses. Intergenerational inequities—future users might potentially pay higher tolls to support current benefits.
Transfer and sharing of project risks to the private sector: • construction cost and schedule, • sufficient traffic and revenue levels, and • increased transparency of project costs.	Not all risks can or should be shared • environmental risks, and • political risks. Potential loss of control: • noncompete provisions, and • toll rate setting.
Secure private sector efficiencies in operations and life-cycle management.	Higher public sector costs: • costs of advisors, • costs of private finance, and potential tax losses.
Obtain a facility that better reflects the true costs of operating and maintaining the facility in setting tolls and better acknowledges the costs and impact to drivers of using the roadway system during times of peak demand. Increase mobility through tolling, congestion pricing, and more efficient decision making.	Risk that the public could pay tolls that are higher than tolls based on the costs of the facilities, including a reasonable rate of return, should a private concessionaire take advantage of market power gained by control of a road for which there are few alternatives that do not require substantially more travel time. Traffic diversion. User equity concerns from tolling.

Source: GAO.

HIGHWAY PUBLIC-PRIVATE PARTNERSHIPS HAVE BEEN USED TO PROVIDE NEW INFRASTRUCTURE AND FUNDING FOR TRANSPORTATION AND OTHER NEEDS AND HAVE THE POTENTIAL TO PROVIDE OTHER BENEFITS

Highway public-private partnerships have resulted in advantages from the perspective of state and local governments, such as the construction of new facilities without the use of public funding and extracting value—in the form of up-front payments—from existing facilities for reinvestment in transportation and other public programs. In addition, highway public-private partnerships can potentially provide other benefits to the public sector, including the transfer of project risks to the private sector, increased operational efficiencies through private sector operation and life-cycle management, and benefits of pricing and improved investment decision making that result from increased use of tolling.

Finance New Construction and Receive up-front Payments through Asset Monetization

In the United States and abroad, public-sector entities have entered highway public-private partnership agreements to finance the construction of new roadways. As we reported in 2004, by relying on private sector sponsorship and investment to build the roads rather than financing the construction themselves, states (1) conserved funding from their highway capital improvement programs for other projects, (2) avoided the up-front costs of borrowing needed to bridge the gap until toll collections became sufficient to pay for the cost of building the roads and paying the interest on the borrowed funds, and (3) avoided the legislative or administrative limits that governed the amount of outstanding debt these states were allowed to have.[10] All of these results were advantages for the states. For example, the TTC is a project that Texas plans to finance, construct, operate, and maintain through various private sector investors. The project is based on competitive bidding and procurement processes, and it will be developed in individual segments as warranted over 50 years.

While relatively new in the United States, leveraging private resources to obtain highway infrastructure is more common abroad. Since the 1960s, Spain has been active in highway public-private partnerships, using approximately 22 toll highway concessions to construct its 3,000-kilometer[11] (approximately 1,860 mile) national road network at little cost to the national government.[12] By keeping the capital costs off the public budget, Spain mitigated budgetary challenges and met macroeconomic criteria for membership in the European Union's Economic Monetary Union. More recently, Australian state governments have entered into highway public-private partnerships with private sector construction firms and lenders to finance and construct several toll highways in Sydney and Melbourne. Officials with the state of Victoria, Australia, have said that government preferences to limit their debt levels, particularly following a severe recession in the early 1990s, would have made construction of these roads difficult without private financing, even though some of the roads had been on transportation plans for several years.

Some governments in the United States and Canada are also using highway public-private partnerships to extract value from existing infrastructure and raise substantial funds for transportation and other purposes. For example, in 2005 the city of Chicago received about $1.8 billion by leasing the Chicago Skyway to a concession consortium of Spanish and Australian companies for 99 years. The city used the lease proceeds to fund various social services; pay off remaining debt on the Chicago Skyway (about $400 million) and some of the city's general obligation debt; and, create a reserve fund which, according to the former Chief Financial Officer of Chicago, generates as much net revenue in annual interest as the highway had generated in annual tolls. By paying off the city's general obligation debt, the city's credit rating improved, thus reducing the cost of debt in the future.

In another example of extracting value from existing infrastructure, the state of Indiana signed a 75-year, $3.8 billion lease of the Indiana Toll Road in 2006 with the same consortium of private sector companies that had leased the Chicago Skyway. The proceeds will primarily be used to fund the governor's 10-year statewide "Major Moves" transportation plan. Indiana officials told us that Indiana was the only state with a fully funded transportation plan for the next 10 years. Indiana also established reserves from the lease proceeds to provide future funding. Finally, the Provincial Government of Ontario, Canada, preceded both of these concession agreements in 1999 when it entered into a long-term lease with a private consortium for the Highway 407 ETR in the Toronto area in exchange for $3.1 billion Canadian dollars (approximately $2.6 billion U.S. dollars in 1999, or $3.2 billion U.S. dollars in 2007).[13] According to Ontario officials, proceeds from the 407 ETR lease were added to the province's general revenue fund but were not dedicated to a long-term investment or other specific capital projects.

Potential Benefits Associated with Transferring Risks

The public sector may also potentially benefit from transferring or sharing risks with the private sector. These risks include project construction and schedule risks. Various government officials told us that because the private sector analyzes its costs, revenues, and risks throughout the life cycle of a project and adheres to scheduled toll increases, it is able to accept large amounts of risk at the outset of a project, although the private sector prices all project risks and bases its final bid proposal, in part, on the level of risk involved.

The transfer of construction cost and schedule risk to the private sector is especially important and valuable, given the incidence of cost and schedule overruns on public projects. Between 1997 and 2003, we and others identified problems with major federally funded highway and bridge projects and with FHWA's oversight of them.[14] We have reported that on many projects for which we could obtain information, costs had increased, sometimes substantially, and that several factors accounted for the increases, including less than reliable initial cost estimates. We further reported that cost containment was not an explicit statutory or regulatory goal of FHWA's oversight and that the agency had done little to ensure that cost containment was an integral part of the states' project management. Since that time both Congress and DOT have taken action to improve the performance of major projects and federal oversight; however, indications of continuing problems remain. In 2004, DOT established a performance goal that 95 percent of major federally funded infrastructure projects would meet cost and schedule milestones established in project or contract agreements, or achieve them within 10 percent of the established milestones. While federally funded aviation and transit projects have met this goal, federally funded highway projects have missed the goal in each of the past 3 years.[15]

Overseas, an example of a successful transfer of construction risk involves the CityLink highway project in Melbourne, Australia. This project faced several challenges during construction, including difficult geological conditions and a tunnel failure, which caused project delays and added costs. According to officials from the government of Victoria, Australia, because construction risks were borne by the private sector, all cost and schedule overruns came at the expense of the private concessionaire, and no additional costs were imposed on the government. Another benefit of highway public-private partnerships related to the costs of construction is that because highway public-private partnership contracts are public and cost and schedule overruns are generally assumed by the private sector, there can be more public transparency about project costs and timelines than under public projects.

Traffic and revenue risks can also be transferred to the private sector. In some highway public-private partnership projects, traffic and revenues have been low, imposing costs on the private sector but not leading to direct costs to the public sector. For example, the Pocahontas Parkway opened to traffic in stages beginning in May 2002. Revenues have been less than projected on this road because traffic has been lower than projected. Virginia used public and private funds for operating and maintaining the Parkway until it had sufficient revenue to repay initial state funds used for construction and pay for the operation and maintenance through tolls. Traffic projections for 2003 indicated there would be about 840,000 transactions per month (about $1.4 million in revenue). However, as of January 2004, traffic was about 400,000 transactions per month (about $630,000 in revenue). In June 2006, under an amended and restated development agreement, a private concessionaire that believed the road was a good long-term investment assumed responsibility for the road for a period of 99 years. The private concessionaire is now responsible for all debt on the Pocahontas Parkway and the risk that revenues on the highway might not be high enough to support all costs. Similarly, in Australia, construction of the Cross City Tunnel in Sydney was privately funded; but, the project began to experience financial problems when actual traffic and revenues were lower than forecasted. Within the first 2 years of operation, the private operator went into receivership. In September 2007, the Cross City Tunnel project was sold to new owners following a competitive tender process. Government officials from New South Wales told us that, as of spring 2007, there had been no costs to the government because the traffic and revenue risks were borne by the private sector.

Potential Efficiencies in Operations and Life-Cycle Management

Highway public-private partnerships may also yield other potential benefits, such as management of assets in ways that may yield efficiencies in operations and life-cycle management that may reduce total project costs over a project's lifetime. For example, in 2004, FHWA reported that, in contrast to traditional highway contracting methods that have sometimes focused on costs of individual project segments, highway public-private partnerships have more flexibility to maximize the use of innovative technologies. Such technologies will lead to increases in quality and the development of faster and less expensive ways to design and build highway facilities. According to DOT, highway public-private partnerships can also reduce project life-cycle costs.[16] For example, in the case of the Chicago Skyway, the private concession company invested in electronic tolling technologies within the first year of taking over management of the Chicago Skyway. This action was taken because, in the long term, the up-front cost of new technologies would be paid off through increased mobility, higher traffic volumes, a reduced need for toll collectors, and decreased congestion at the toll plaza by increasing traffic throughput. According to the Assistant Budget Director for Chicago, the high initial cost for installing electronic tolling was likely a prohibiting factor for the city to make the same investment, based on the city's limited annual budget. Foreign officials with whom we spoke also identified life-cycle costing and management as a primary benefit of highway public-private partnerships.

Highway public-private partnerships can also better ensure more predictable funding for maintenance and capital repairs of the highway. Under more traditional publicly financed and operated highways, operations and maintenance and capital improvement costs are subject to annual appropriations cycles. This increases the risk that adequate funds may or may not be available to public agencies. However, under a highway public-private partnership, concessionaires are generally held, through contractual provisions, to maintain the highway up to a certain level of standard (sometimes as good as or better than a state would hold itself to) throughout the course of the concession, and the concessionaire must fund all maintenance costs itself. Furthermore, capital improvements, including possible roadway expansions, may also be contractually required of concessionaires ensuring that such works will be conducted as needed. Finally, the desire for a safe and well-maintained roadway in order to attract traffic (and, therefore, revenues) may incentivize a private operator to useful and efficient operations and maintenance techniques and practices.

Potential Pricing and Investment Decision-Making Benefits

Highway public-private partnerships can also potentially provide mobility and other benefits to the public sector, through the use of tolling. The highway public-private partnerships we reviewed all involved toll roads. Highway public-private partnerships potentially provide benefits by better pricing infrastructure to reflect the true costs of operating and maintaining the facility and thus realizing public benefits of improved condition and performance of public infrastructure. In addition, through the use of tolling, highway public-private partnerships can use tolling techniques designed to have drivers readily understand the full cost of decisions to use the road system during times of peak demand and potentially reduce the demand for roads during peak hours. Through congestion pricing, tolls can be set to vary during congested periods to maintain a predetermined level of service. Such tolls create financial incentives for drivers to consider costs when making their driving decisions. In response, drivers may choose to share rides, use transit, travel at less congested (generally off-peak) times, or travel on less congested routes to reduce their toll payments. Such choices can potentially reduce congestion and the demand for road space at peak periods, thus allowing the capacity of existing roadways to accommodate demand with fewer delays. For example, a representative of the government of Ontario, Canada, told us that the 407 ETR helped relieve congestion in Toronto by attracting traffic from a parallel publicly financed untolled highway. In fact, advisors to the government said that the officials established a tolling schedule for the 407 ETR based on achieving predetermined optimal traffic flows on the 407 ETR.

Tolling can also potentially lead to targeted, rational, and efficient investment decisions. National roadway policy has long incorporated the user pays concept, according to which roadway users pay the costs of building and maintaining roadways, generally in the form of excise taxes on motor fuels and other taxes on inputs into driving, such as taxes on tires or fees for registering vehicles or obtaining operator licenses. Increasingly, however, decision makers have looked to other revenue sources—including income, property, and sales tax revenues—to finance roads in ways that do not adhere to the user pays principle. Tolling, however, is more consistent with user pay principles because tolling a particular road and using the toll revenues collected to build and maintain that road more closely aligns the costs with the distribution of the benefits that users derive from it. Furthermore, roadway investment can be more efficient when it is financed by tolls because the users who benefit will likely support additional investment to build new capacity or enhance existing capacity only when they believe the benefits exceed the costs. In addition, toll project construction is typically financed by bonds sold and backed by future toll revenues, and projects must pass the test of market viability and meet goals demanded by investors, thus better ensuring that there is sufficient demand for roads financed through tolling. However, even with this test there is no guarantee that projects will always be viable.

Potential Private Sector Benefits

The private sector, and in particular, private investment groups, including equity funds and pension fund managers, have recently demonstrated an increasing interest in investing in public infrastructure. They see the sector as representing long-term assets with stable, potentially high yield returns. While these private sector investors may benefit from highway public-private partnerships, they can also lose money through a highway public-private partnership. Although profits are generally not realized in the first 10 to 15 years of a concession agreement, the private sector receives benefits from highway public-private partnerships over the term of a concession in the form of a return on its investment.[17] Private sector investors generally finance large public sector benefits early in a concession period, including up-front payments for leases of existing projects or capital outlays for the construction of new, large-scale transportation projects. In return, the private sector expects to recover any and all up-front costs (whether construction costs of new facilities or concession fees paid to the public sector for existing facilities), as well as ongoing maintenance and operation costs, and generate a return on investment. According to investment firms with whom we spoke, future toll revenue from tolled transportation projects can provide reliable long-term investment opportunities. Furthermore, any cost savings or operational efficiencies the private sector can generate, such as introducing electronic tolling, improving maintenance practices, or increasing customer satisfaction in other ways can further boost the return on investment through increased traffic flow and increased toll revenue.

The private sector can also receive potential tax deductions from depreciation on assets involving private sector investment and the availability of these deductions were important incentives to the private sector to enter some of the highway public-private partnerships we reviewed. Obtaining these deductions, however, may require lengthy concessions periods. In the United States, federal tax law allows private concessionaires to claim income tax deductions for depreciation on a facility (whether new highways or existing highways obtained through a concession) if the concessionaire has effective ownership of the property. Effective ownership requires, among other things, that the length of a concession be greater than or equal to the useful economic life of the asset. Financial and legal experts, including those who were involved in the Chicago and Indiana transactions, told us that since the concession lengths of the Chicago Skyway and the Indiana Toll Road agreements each exceed their useful life, the private investors can claim full tax deductions for asset depreciation within the first 15 years of the lease agreement.[18] The requirement to demonstrate effective asset ownership contributed to the 99-year and 75-year concession terms for the Chicago Skyway and Indiana Toll Road, respectively. One tax expert told us that, in general, infrastructure assets (such as highways) obtained by the private sector in a highway public-private partnership may be depreciated on an accelerated basis over a 15-year period.[19]

Private investors can also potentially benefit from being able to use tax-exempt financing authorized by SAFETEA-LU in 2005. Private activity bonds have been provided for private sector use to generate proceeds that are then used to construct new highway facilities under highway public-private partnerships.[20] This exemption lowers private sector costs in financing highway public-private partnership projects. As of January 2008, DOT had approved private activity bonds for 5 projects totaling $3.2 billion[21] and had applications pending for 3 projects totaling $2.2 billion. DOT said it expects applications for private activity bond allocations from an additional 12 projects totaling more than $10 billion in 2008.

Finally, the private sector can potentially benefit through gains achieved in refinancing their investments. Both public and private sector officials with whom we spoke agreed that refinancing is common in highway public-private partnerships. Refinancing may occur early in a concession period as the initial investors either attempt to "cash out" their investment—that is, sell their investment to others and use the proceeds for other investment opportunities—or obtain new, lower cost financing for the existing investment. Refinancing may also be used to reduce the initial equity investment in highway public-private partnerships. Refinancing gains can occur throughout a concession period; as project risks typically decrease after construction, the project may outperform expectations, or there may be a general decrease in interest rates. In the case of the Chicago Skyway, the concession company had to secure a large amount of money in a short period of time to close on the agreement with the city. According to the Chief Executive Officer of the Skyway Concession Company, the company obtained a loan package with the best interest rates available at the time and refinanced within 7 months of financial close on the agreement. He said this refinance resulted in a better deal, including better leverage and interest rates.[22] An investment banker involved in the Chicago Skyway concession told us that refinancing plans are often incorporated into the original investment business case and form an important part of each bidders' competitive offer. For example, if the toll road is not refinanced, the investment will underperform against its original business case. The investment banker said that there was no refinancing gain on the Chicago Skyway because the gain was already planned for as part of the initial investment case and was reflected in the financial offer to the city of Chicago. In some cases, refinancing gains may not be anticipated or incorporated into the financial offer and may be realized later in a concession period. The governments of the United Kingdom and Victoria and New South Wales, Australia, have acknowledged that gains generated from lower cost financing can be substantial, and they now require as a provision in each privately financed contract that any refinancing gains achieved by concessionaires—and not already factored into the calculation of tolls—be shared equally with the government. For example, the state of Victoria, Australia, shared in refinancing gains from the private investor's refinancing of a highway public-private partnership project in Melbourne called EastLink project.

Highway Public-Private Partnerships May Not Be Applicable to All Situations

Highway public-private partnerships may not be applicable to all situations, given the challenges of tolling and the private sector's need to make profits. While tolling has promise as an approach to enhance mobility and finance transportation, officials face many challenges in obtaining public and political support for implementing tolling. As we reported in June 2006, based on interviews with 49 state departments of transportation, opposition to tolling stems from the contention that fuel taxes and other dedicated funding sources are used to pay for roads, and thus tolling is seen as a form of double taxation.[23] In addition, concerns about equity are often raised, including the potential unequal ability of lower-income and higher-income groups to pay tolls, as well the use of tolling to address the transportation needs in one part of a state while freeing up federal and state funding in tolled areas to address transportation needs in another part of a state.[24] State officials also face practical challenges in implementing tolling, including obtaining the statutory authority to toll and addressing the traffic diversion that might result when motorists seek to avoid toll facilities. Our June 2006 report concluded that state and local governments may be able to address these concerns by (1) honestly and forthrightly addressing the challenges that a tolling approach presents, (2) pursuing strategies that focus on developing an institutional framework that facilitates tolling, (3) demonstrating leadership, and (4) pursuing toll projects that provide tangible benefits to users.

Although highway public-private partnerships could conceivably be used for reconstructing existing roadways, in practice this could be very difficult, due, in part, to public and political opposition to tolling existing free roads. Aside from bridges and tunnels, existing Interstate Highway System roads generally cannot be tolled, except under specific pilot programs. One such program, the Interstate System Reconstruction and Rehabilitation Pilot Program, was authorized in 1998 to permit three states to toll existing interstate highways to finance major reconstruction or rehabilitation needs. Two states applied for and received preliminary approval to do so—Virginia in 2003 and Missouri in 2005—and

Pennsylvania submitted an application in 2007. While Virginia's toll project is proceeding through environmental review, Missouri's project remains on hold, and Pennsylvania's application awaits approval. In addition, three other states submitted applications and withdrew them, owing in part to public and political opposition to tolls. A fourth state sent in an "Expression of Interest" for this pilot program, but the state never formally submitted an application. An official with the metropolitan planning organization for Chicago said tolling highways is difficult in Illinois, especially when the public is use to free alternatives, and an official with the California DOT echoed this sentiment, saying that highway public-private partnerships are not a substitute or final solution for ongoing funding of transportation infrastructure. FHWA officials agreed that highway public-private partnerships are not suitable in all situations.

Another reason highway public-private partnerships may not be applicable to all situations is that the private sector has a profit motive and is likely to only enter highway public-private partnerships for new construction projects that are expected to produce an adequate rate of return on investment. Therefore, highway public-private partnerships appear to be most suited for construction of new infrastructure in areas where congestion may be a problem and traffic is expected to be sufficient to generate net profits through toll revenues. For example, we found that Oregon has decided to forego a highway public-private partnership for one possible highway public-private partnership project in the Portland area because the forecasted revenues were not high enough to make the route toll viable for private investors. Similarly, Texas has concluded that not all segments of the TTC are toll viable; these segments might not receive direct private interest and might need to be subsidized with concession fees from other segments or other funds, including public dollars, if they are available. According to the Texas DOT, some projects will be partially toll viable and may require both public and private funds. DOT officials told us that, in both Oregon and Texas, funds are currently not available to procure these projects through a public procurement.

Highway Public-Private Partnerships Also Come with Potential Costs and Trade-offs to the Public Sector

Highway public-private partnerships come with potential costs and trade-offs to the public sector. The costs include the potential for higher user tolls than under public toll roads and potentially more expensive project costs than publicly procured projects. While the public sector can benefit through the transfer or sharing of some project risks with the private sector, not all risks can or should be transferred; and, the public sector may lose some control through a highway public-private partnership. Finally, because there are many stakeholders with interests in a public-private partnership as well as many potential objectives—and many governments affected—there are trade-offs in protecting the public interest.

Potential Financial Costs and Trade-offs

Although highway public-private partnerships can be used to obtain financing for highway infrastructure without the use of public sector funding, there is no "free money" in highway public-private partnerships. Rather, this funding is a form of privately issued debt that must be repaid. Private concessionaires primarily make a return on their investment by collecting toll revenues. Though concession agreements can limit the extent to which a concessionaire can raise tolls, it is likely that tolls will increase on a privately operated highway to a greater extent than they would on a publicly run toll road. For example, during the time the Chicago Skyway was publicly managed, tolls changed infrequently and actually decreased by approximately [25] percent in real terms (2007 dollars) between 1989 and 2004 (see figure 5). According to the former Chief Financial Officer of Chicago, the Chicago Skyway had not historically increased its tolls unless required by law, even though the Skyway had been operating at a loss and had outstanding debt. On the other hand, under private control, maximum tolls are generally set in accordance with concession agreements and, in contrast to public sector practices, allowable toll increases can be frequent and automatic. The concession agreements for both the Chicago Skyway and Indiana Toll Road permit toll rates to increase each year, based on a minimum of 2 percent and a maximum of the annual change of either the CPI or per capita U.S. nominal gross domestic product (GDP), whichever is higher.25 Based on estimated increases in nominal gross domestic product and population, the tolls on the Chicago Skyway will be permitted to increase in real terms nearly 97 percent from 2007 through 2047—from $2.50 to $4.91 in 2007 dollars.[26] This is also shown in figure 5. These future toll projections reflect the maximum allowable toll rates, which have been authorized by the public sector in the concession agreements.

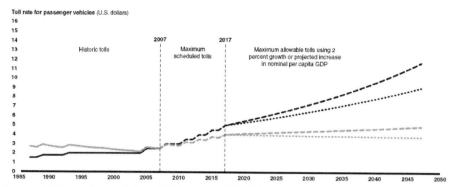

Source: GAO analysis of city of Chicago and OECD data.

Note: Historical data are from 1986 to 2006; scheduled maximum toll rates are from 2007 to 2017; and projected toll rates from 2008 to 2047. Projections to 2047 are based on 2 percent growth, or forecasted per capita GDP growth, adjusted to 2007 dollars.

Figure 5. Change in Chicago Skyway Tolls, 1967 to 2047.

Depending on market conditions, the potential exists that the public could pay higher tolls than those that would more appropriately reflect the true costs of operating and maintaining the facilities, including earning a reasonable rate of return. Within the maximum allowable toll rates authorized by the public sector in the concession agreements, toll rate changes will be driven by such market factors as the demand for travel on the road, which, in turn, will be influenced by the level of competition that toll road concessionaires will face. This competition will vary from facility to facility. In cases where an untolled public roadway or other transportation mode (e.g., bus or rail) is a viable travel alternative to the toll road, these competing alternatives may act to constrain toll rates. In other instances, where there are not other viable travel alternatives to a toll road that would not require substantially more travel time, there may be few constraints on toll rates other than the terms of the concession. In such instances, a concessionaire may have substantial market power, which could give the concessionaire the ability to set toll rates that exceed the costs of the toll road, including a reasonable rate of return, as long as those toll rates are below the maximum rates allowed by the concession agreement. We have not determined the extent to which any concessionaire would have substantial market power due to limited alternatives, although this is an appropriate consideration when entering possible highway public-private partnerships.

In addition to potentially higher tolls, the public sector may give up more than it receives in a concession payment in using a highway public-private partnership with a focus on extracting value from an existing facility. Conversely, because the private sector takes on substantial risks, the opposite could also be true—that is, the public sector might gain more than it gives up. In exchange for an up-front concession payment, the public sector gives up control over a future stream of toll revenues over an extended period of time, such as 75 or 99 years. It is possible that the net present value of the future stream of toll revenues (less operating and capital costs) given up can be much larger than the concession payment received. Concession payments could potentially be less than they could or should be. In Indiana the state hired an accounting and consulting firm to conduct a study of the net present value of the Indiana Toll Road and deemed its value to the state to be slightly under $2 billion. This valuation assumed that future toll increases would be similar to the past—infrequent and in line with the road's history under public control. An alternative valuation of the toll road lease performed by an economics professor on behalf of opponents of the concession changed certain assumptions of the net present value model and produced a different result—about $11 billion. This valuation assumed annual toll rate increases by the public authority of 4.4 percent, compared with the 2.8 percent used in the state's valuation.[27] We did not evaluate this study and make no conclusions about its validity; other studies may have reached different conclusions; however, the results of this study illustrate how toll rate assumptions can influence asset valuations and, therefore, expected concession payments.

Similarly, unforeseen circumstances can dramatically alter the relative value of future revenues compared with the market value of the facility. In 1999, the government of Ontario, Canada received a $3.1 billion concession fee in exchange for the long-term lease for the 407 ETR. In the years following the concession agreement, as commercial and residential development along the 407 ETR corridor exceeded initial government projections, the value of the roadway increased. In 2002, a valuation conducted by an investor in the concession estimated that the market value of the facility had nearly doubled—from $3.1 billion Canadian to $6.2 billion Canadian. This valuation included a new 40 kilometers that had been added to the 407 ETR since it was originally built, as well as additional parking lots and increased tolls.

Using a highway public-private partnership to extract value from an existing facility also raises issues about the use of those proceeds and whether future users might potentially pay higher tolls to support current benefits. In some instances, up-front payments have been used for immediate needs, and it remains to be seen whether these uses provide long-term benefits to future generations who will potentially be paying progressively higher toll rates to the private sector throughout the length of a concession agreement. Both Chicago and Indiana used their lease fees, in part, to fund immediate financial needs. Chicago, for example, used lease proceeds to finance various city programs, while Indiana used lease proceeds primarily to fund its "Major Moves" 10-year transportation program. However, Chicago also used the proceeds to retire both Chicago Skyway and some city debt, and both Chicago and Indiana established long-term reserves from the lease proceeds. Conversely, proceeds from the lease of Highway 407 ETR in Toronto, Canada, went into the province's general revenue fund, and officials in the Ministry of Transport were unaware of how the payment was spent. Consequently, it is not clear if those uses of proceeds will benefit future roadway users.

Highway public-private partnerships also potentially require additional costs to the public sector compared with traditional public procurement. These costs include potential additional costs associated with (1) required financial and legal advisors, and (2) private sector financing compared with public sector financing. A June 2007 study by the University of Southern California found that because the U.S. transportation sector has little experience with long-term concession agreements, state departments of transportation are unlikely to have in-house expertise needed to plan, conduct, and execute highway public-private partnerships. FHWA has also recognized this issue—in a 2006 report it noted that, in several states, promising projects have been delayed for lack of staff capacity and expertise to confidently conclude agreements. Furthermore, public sector agencies must also exercise diligence to prevent potential conflicts of interest, if the legal and financial firms also advise private investors. In addition, highway public-private partnership projects are likely to have the higher cost of private finance because public sector agencies generally have access to tax-exempt debt, while private companies generally do not.

Financial trade-offs can also involve federal tax issues. As discussed earlier, unlike public toll authorities, the private sector pays income taxes to the federal government and the ability to deduct depreciation on assets involved with highway public-private partnerships for which they have effective ownership for tax purposes can reduce that tax obligation. The extent of these deductions and amounts of foregone revenue, if any, to the federal or state governments are difficult to determine, since they depend on such factors as the taxable income, total deductions, and marginal tax rates of private sector entities involved with highway public-private partnerships. Nevertheless, foregone revenue can also amount to millions of dollars.[28] For example, there may be foregone tax revenue when the private sector uses tax-exempt private activity bonds. As we reported in 2004, the 2003 cost to the federal government from tax-exempt bonds used to finance three projects with private sector involvement—Pocahontas Parkway, Southern Connector, and the Las Vegas Monorail—was between $25 million and $35 million.[29] There can also be potential costs of highway public-private partnerships using public finance since state and local debt is also tax deductible. Regardless of the tax impact on government revenues, the availability of depreciation deductions can be important to private sector concessionaires. As discussed earlier, financial experts with whom we spoke said that depreciation deductions associated with the Chicago Skyway and Indiana Toll Road transactions were significant, and that it is likely that in the absence of the depreciation benefit, the concession payments to Chicago and Indiana would have been less than $1.8 and $3.8 billion, respectively.

Potential Loss of Control

In highway public-private partnerships the public sector may lose some control over its ability to modify existing assets or implement plans to accommodate changes over time. For example, concession agreements may contain noncompete provisions designed to limit competition from or elicit compensation for highways or other transportation facilities that may compete and draw traffic from a leased toll road. The case of SR-91 in California illustrates an early and extreme example of a noncompete provision's potential effect. In 1991, the California DOT used a highway public-private partnership to construct express lanes in the middle of the existing SR-91. The express lanes were owned and operated by a private concessionaire, and the public sector continued to own the adjacent lanes. The concession contained provisions that prevented improvements or expansions of the adjacent public lanes. Eight years after signing the concession agreement, the local transportation authority purchased the concessionaire's rights to the tolled express lanes, thus enabling transportation improvements to be made.[30] It appears that noncompete clauses in projects that followed SR-91 have generally provided more flexibility to modify nearby existing roads and build new infrastructure when necessary. This issue is discussed further in the next section of the chapter.

The public sector may also lose some control of toll rate setting by entering into highway public-private partnerships. Highway public-private partnership agreements generally allow the private operator to raise tolls in accordance with provisions outlined in the concession contract. The private operator may be able to raise tolls on an annual basis, without prior approval. To the extent that the public sector may want to adjust toll rates—for example, to manage demand on their highway network—they may be unable to do so because the toll setting capability is defined exclusively by the concession contract and the private operator.

Not All Risks Can or Should Be Transferred in Highway Public-Private Partnerships

While the public sector may benefit from the transfer of risk in a highway public-private partnership, not all risks can or should be transferred and there may be trade-offs. There are costs and risks associated with environmental issues, which often cannot or should not be transferred to the private sector in a highway public-private partnership. For example, if a project is to be eligible for federal funds at any point throughout the project lifetime, a lengthy environmental review process must be completed, as required for all federally funded projects, by the National Environmental Policy Act (NEPA). There can also be various federal permits and approvals required. The financial risk associated with the environmental assessment process (and whether the project will be approved) generally resides with the public sector, in part, because the environmental review process can add to project costs and can cause significant project delays. In addition, the private sector may be unwilling to accept the risk and project uncertainty associated with the publicly controlled environmental review process. An example of the delay that can be experienced in projects undergoing environmental review includes the South Bay Expressway in California. The state selected a private sponsor for this project in 1991. However, litigation challenging the final record of decision on the environmental impact statement for the project was not resolved until March 2003, and construction did not begin until July 2003. In another example, private sector officials in Texas have told us they are not involved with the environmental assessment process for the TTC, given the added costs and the increased project delivery times. According to the Texas DOT, environmental review is a core function of government and a risk that to date appears best suited to the public sector.

Finally, there may also be political trade-offs faced by the public sector when involved in highway public-private partnerships. For example, public opposition to the TTC and other highway public-private partnerships in Texas remains strong. Although the governor of Texas has identified a lack of funds as a barrier to meeting the state's transportation needs, public outcry over the TTC and the lack of involvement of local governments was so substantial that in June 2007 the state legislature enacted a 2-year moratorium on future highway public-private partnerships in the state.[31] In the case of the 407 ETR in Toronto, a consultant to the Ontario Ministry of Transportation told us the government was publicly criticized for the transaction and road users had little understanding of the reasons the government entered the agreements or what the future toll rates could be. As a result, the government suffered public backlash. Similarly, the New South Wales government, as part of its agreement with the concession company of the Cross City Tunnel in Sydney, Australia, closed some city streets in order to mitigate local congestion in the downtown area as part of the tunnel project. Although the government's intent was to alleviate congestion from downtown Sydney, many drivers felt that they were diverted into the tolled tunnel, and the government was criticized for its actions.

It Is Important to Consider the Opportunities of Highway Public-Private Partnerships Against Public Objectives, Potential Costs, and Trade-offs, as well as Public Interests

The diversity and uncertainty of both the benefits and costs of highway public-private partnerships of the type we reviewed—long-term concessions—are complex and suggest that the merits of future partnerships will need careful evaluation on a case-by-case basis. As noted above, highway public-private partnerships have the potential to provide benefits, such as construction of new facilities, without the use of public finance, the transfer or sharing of project risks, and achievement of increased operational efficiencies through private sector operation and life-cycle management. However, also as discussed earlier, there are costs and trade-offs involved, including loss of public-sector control of toll setting and potentially more expensive project costs than publicly procured projects. State and local governments pursue highway public-private partnerships to achieve specific public objectives, such as congestion relief and mobility or increasing freight mobility. In some instances, the potential benefits of highway public-private partnerships may outweigh the potential costs and trade-offs, and the use of highway public-private partnerships and long-term concessions would serve the public well into the future. In other instances, the potential costs and trade-offs may outweigh the potential benefits, and the public interest may not be well served by using such an arrangement. In instances where public officials choose to go with a highway public-private partnership accomplished through a long-term concession, realizing potential benefits will require careful structuring of the public-private partnership agreement and identifying and mitigating the direct risks of the project.

From a public perspective, an important component of any analysis of potential benefits and costs of highway public-private partnerships and long-term concessions is consideration of the public interest. As with any highway project, there can be many stakeholders in highway public-private partnerships, each of which may have its own interests. Stakeholders include regular toll road users, commercial truck and bus drivers, emergency response vehicles, toll road employees, and members of the public who may be affected by ancillary effects of a highway public-private partnership, including users of nearby roads, land owners, special interest groups and taxpayers, in general (see figure 6).

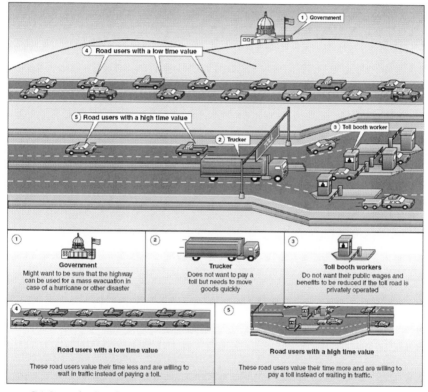

Source: GAO analysis of FHWA data.

Figure 6. Various Stakeholder Interests Associated with Highway Public-Private Partnerships.

Identification of the public interest is a function of scale and can differ based on the range of stakeholders and the geographic and political domain considered. At the national level, the public interest may include facilitating interstate commerce, as well as meeting mobility needs. State and regional public interest, however, might prioritize new infrastructure to meet local demand or maximum up-front payments to reduce debt or finance transportation plans above and beyond national mobility objectives. With competing interests over the duration of the concession agreement, trade-offs will be necessary. For example, if mobility is an objective of the project, high toll rates at times of peak travel demand may be necessary to deter some users from driving during peak hours and thus mitigate congestion. But, if rates are too high, traffic diversion to free alternate public routes may be an unintended outcome that could adversely affect drivers on those roads.

HIGHWAY PUBLIC-PRIVATE PARTNERSHIPS HAVE SOUGHT TO PROTECT PUBLIC INTEREST IN MANY WAYS, BUT USE OF PUBLIC INTEREST CRITERIA IS MIXED IN THE UNITED STATES

The public interest in highway public-private partnerships can and has been considered and protected in many ways. State and local officials in the projects we reviewed heavily relied on concession terms. Most often, these terms were focused on ensuring performance of the asset, dealing with financial issues such as toll rates, maintaining the public sector's accountability and flexibility to provide transportation services to the public, addressing workforce issues, and maintaining the ability to address these concession terms over the life of the contract. Additionally, oversight and monitoring mechanisms were used to ensure that private partners fulfill their obligations. In addition to concession terms, certain financial analyses were used to protect the public interest. For example, PSCs, which attempt to compare estimated project costs as a highway public-private partnership with undertaking a project publicly, have been used for some highway projects. We found that some foreign governments have also used formal public interest tools as well as public interest criteria tests. However, use of these tests and tools has been more limited in the United States. Not using formal public interest criteria and assessment tools can potentially allow aspects of the public interest to be overlooked and use of formal analyses before entering into highway public-private partnerships can help lay out the expected benefits and costs of the project.

Highway Public-Private Partnerships We Reviewed Have Used Concession Terms to Protect the Public Interest

The highway public-private partnerships we reviewed have used various mechanisms to protect the public interest by holding concessionaires to requirements related to such things as performance of an asset, financial aspects of agreements, the public sector's ability to remain accountable as a provider of public goods and services, workforce protections, and concession oversight. Because agreeing to these terms may make an asset less valuable to the private sector, public sector agencies might have accepted lower payments in return for these terms.

Asset Performance Measures

Public sector agencies involved in highway public-private partnerships have attempted to protect the public interest by ensuring that the performance of the asset is upheld to high safety, maintenance, and operational standards and can be expanded when necessary (see table 3). Operating and maintenance standards were incorporated in the Indiana Toll Road and Chicago Skyway concession agreements. Based on documents we reviewed, the standards on the Indiana Toll Road detail how the concessionaire must maintain the road's condition, utility, and level of safety with the intent to ensure that the public would not see any reduction in the performance of the highway over the 75-year lease term. The standards also detail how the concessionaire must address a wide range of roadway issues, such as signage, use of safety features such as barrier walls, snow and ice removal, and the level of pavement smoothness that must be maintained. According to a Deputy Commissioner with the Indiana DOT, the standards actually hold the lessee to a higher level of performance than when the state operated the highway, because the state did not have the funding to maintain the Indiana Toll Road to its own standards. For the Chicago Skyway, the concessionaire is required to follow detailed maintenance and operations standards that are based on industry best practices and address maintenance issues such as roadway maintenance, drainage maintenance, and roadway safety features, as well as operational issues such as toll collection procedures, emergency planning, and snow and ice control procedures. According to an engineering consultant with the city of Chicago who was involved in writing the standards used in the concession, when the Chicago Skyway had been under public control, employees were not required to follow formal standards.

Table 3. Selected Performance Mechanisms to Protect the Public Interest

Issue	Project	Details
Detailed operating and maintenance standards	Chicago Skyway	The concessionaire must follow detailed technical and operational specifications based on industry best practices that address maintenance issues such as roadway maintenance, drainage maintenance, and roadway safety features, as well as operational issues such as toll collection procedures, emergency planning, and snow removal.
Expansion triggers	Indiana Toll Road	Concessionaire must act to improve Level of Service (LOS) on Indiana Toll Road when Level of Service[a] forecasted to reach Level C in rural areas or Level D in urban areas.

Source: GAO analysis of concession contracts.

[a] LOS is a measure of traffic congestion. In LOS C, the influence of traffic density becomes marked and the ability to maneuver within the traffic stream is affected by other vehicles. In LOS D, the ability to maneuver is severely restricted due to traffic congestion and travel speed is reduced by the increasing volume of traffic.

Concessions may include requirements to maintain performance in terms of mobility and capacity by ensuring a certain level of traffic throughput and avoiding congestion. Highway public-private partnerships may also require that a concessionaire expand a facility once congestion reaches a certain level and some agreements can include capacity and expansion triggers based on LOS forecasts. LOS is a qualitative measure of congestion; according to the concession agreement, on the Indiana Toll Road, when LOS is forecasted to fall below certain levels within 7 years, the concessionaire must act to improve the LOS, such as by adding additional capacity (such as an extra lane) at its own cost, to ease the future projected congestion. Because the provisions call for expansions in advance of poor mobility conditions, it appears this agreement aims to prevent a high level of congestion from ever happening. According to Texas DOT officials, the concessionaire for the State Highway 130, segments 5 and 6 project (see table 1) will be required to add capacity through expansion, or better manage traffic, to improve traffic flow if the average speed of vehicles on the roadway falls below a predetermined level. According to government officials in Toronto, Canada, the private operator of the 407 ETR is also required to maintain a certain vehicle flow and traffic growth on the road or face financial penalties.

Financial Mechanisms

Public sector agencies have also sought to protect the public interest in highway public-private partnerships through financial mechanisms such as toll rate setting limitations (see table 4). However, the toll limitations used in U.S. highway public-private partnerships that we reviewed may be sufficiently generous to the private sector that they might not effectively limit toll increases. Toll limitations constrain the high profit-maximizing toll levels that a private concessionaire might otherwise set. As discussed earlier, tolls on the Chicago Skyway can be increased at predetermined levels for the first 12 years of the lease (rising from $2.50 to $5 per 2-axle vehicle). Afterward, tolls can then increase annually at the highest of three factors: 2 percent, increase in CPI, or increase in nominal per capita GDP. According to the concession agreement, tolls on the Indiana Toll Road can be increased at set levels until mid-2010 and then can rise by a minimum of 2 percent or a maximum of the prior year's increase in CPI or nominal per capita GDP. In general, these limitations are meant to restrict the rate of toll increases over time. Since nominal GDP has generally increased at an annual rate of between 4 and 7 percent over the last 20 years, the restrictions may not effectively limit toll increases.

Some foreign governments have taken a different approach to limiting toll increases that may create more constraining limits. For example, in Spain, we were told that concessionaires are limited to increasing tolls by roughly the rate of inflation in Spain every year (although slight adjustments may be made based on traffic levels). In contrast, since the annual rate of inflation in the United States has typically been lower than nominal GDP growth (except during years of negative real GDP change), the maximum allowable toll increases in Chicago and Indiana will likely exceed the U.S. inflation rate. We were told that in the EastLink project in Australia, toll rates have been kept low by having prospective bidders for a concession bid down the level of toll rates; the contract is awarded to the bidder that agrees to operate the facility with the lowest toll. Government officials told us that this process resulted in the lowest per kilometer toll rate of any toll road in Australia. However, using a process that constrains bidders to the lowest tolls may involve government subsidies. Although no closure of competing roads or government subsidies were involved with the EastLink project in Victoria, Australia, the potential for government subsidies was involved in the Cross City Tunnel project in Sydney, Australia. An official with the New South Wales government said the government was adopting a new policy in light of the Cross City Tunnel project specifying that the government should be prepared to provide subsidies on toll road projects to keep tolls at certain predetermined levels. In commenting on a draft of this chapter, DOT officials said that different government agencies may have different goals for highway public-private partnerships besides keeping tolls low. These other goals could include maximizing the number of new facilities provided, earning the largest up-front payment or annual revenue sharing, or using higher tolls to maximize mobility and choice.

Revenue-sharing mechanisms have also been used to protect the public interest by requiring a concessionaire to share some level of revenues with the public sector. For example, in Texas, revenues on the State Highway 130, segments 5 and 6, concession will be shared with the state so that the higher the return on investment of the private concessionaire, the higher the share with the state. For example, after a one-time, up-front payment of $25 million, if the annual return on investment of the private concessionaire is at or below 11 percent, then the state could share in 5 percent of all revenues. If it is over 15 percent, then Texas could receive 50 percent of the net revenues. Higher returns would warrant higher revenue shares for the state. Officials with the Texas DOT said they see revenue sharing, as opposed to one large up-front payment at lease signing, as protecting the public interest in the long run and ensuring that the public and private sectors share common goals. Both Chicago and Indiana officials told us there were no revenue sharing arrangements in either the Chicago Skyway or Indiana Toll Road concessions.

Table 4. Selected Financial Mechanisms to Protect the Public Interest

Type of control	Project	Details
Revenue sharing	TTC	Based on return on investment of concessionaire.
Toll rate limitations	Indiana Toll Road	Fixed increases until mid-2010, afterwards allowed annual increase of the higher of 2 percent, nominal per capita GDP growth, or CPI growth.

Source: GAO analysis of Indiana and Texas data.

Foreign governments have also used other financial mechanisms, such as controls on public subsidies to private projects and the sharing of refinancing gains, to protect the public interest in highway public-private partnerships. For example, in Spain, we were told that concessionaires for highway projects that require public subsidies often bid for the lowest subsidy possible to lower costs to the government. In other highway projects, the government of Spain will provide loans for private projects for which the interest rate on repayment is based on traffic levels: the lower the traffic level the lower the interest rate. According to documents we reviewed, in highway public-private partnerships in both Victoria and New South Wales, Australia, any profits the concessionaire earns by refinancing of the asset must be shared with the government. In May 2007, the government of New South Wales, Australia, issued guidance in relation to refinancing gains.[32] According to a New South Wales official, the general position of the government on highway public-private partnership refinancing is that all refinancings, other than those contemplated at financial close, require government consent. Government consent plays a fundamental role in project refinancing since refinancing may increase project risk by increasing debt burden and reducing investors' long-term financial incentives, among other things. In Canada, federal policy requires that any federal funds used to construct a road that is then leased to a private concessionaire must be repaid to the federal government.

Accountability and Flexibility

Governments entering into highway public-private partnerships have also acted to protect the public interest by ensuring that they are not fully constrained by the concession and are still able to provide transportation infrastructure (see table 5). This flexibility has been achieved in part by avoiding fully restrictive noncompete clauses. Since Orange County bought back the SR-91 managed lanes because it was no longer willing to be bound by the restrictive noncompete clause it originally agreed to, governments entering into highway public-private partnerships have sought to avoid such restrictive clauses.[33] Some more recent noncompete clauses can be referred to as "compensation clauses" because they require that the public sector compensate the concessionaire if the public sector proceeds (in certain instances) with an unplanned project that might take revenues from the concessionaire's toll road. For example, for the State Highway 130 concession in Texas, both the positive and negative impacts that new public roads will have on the toll road will be determined and, potentially, Texas DOT will compensate the concessionaire for losses of revenues on the concession toll road. However, that payment might be counterbalanced by Texas DOT receiving credits for new publicly constructed roads that are demonstrated to increase traffic on the concession toll road. Additionally, according to the Texas DOT, on the State Highway 130 concession, projects already on the state's 20-year transportation plan when the concession was signed are exempt from any such provisions. Certain other projects are also exempt, such as expansions or safety improvements made to I-35 (a parallel existing highway on the Interstate Highway System); any local, city, or county improvements; or, any multimodal rail projects. According to the Texas DOT, in no case is it, or any other governmental authority, precluded from building necessary infrastructure. A noncompete clause lowers potential competition from other roadways for a private concessionaire, thereby increasing their potential revenues. Therefore, a contract without any noncompete provisions, all else equal, is likely to attract lower concession payments from the private sector.

Table 5. Selected Noncompete Provisions

Project/site	Details
Texas	Compensation clause—State must compensate concessionaire for loss of revenues resulting from new construction; projects on existing transportation plans are exempt.
Indiana	Clause prevents state from building a highway of 20 or more miles in length that is within 10 miles of the Indiana Toll Road; all other work is allowed.
Chicago Skyway	No noncompete clause.

Source: GAO analysis of selected highway public-private partnership contracts.

According to an Indiana official, a noncompete clause for the Indiana Toll Road requires the state to compensate the concessionaire an amount equal to the concessionaire's lost revenue from a new highway if the state constructs a new interstate quality highway with 20 or more continuous miles within 10 miles of the Indiana Toll Road. Indiana officials told us that the concession agreement for the Indiana Toll Road does not prevent the state from building competing facilities and provides great latitude in maintaining and expanding the state's transportation network around the toll road and that they do not expect this restriction to place serious constraints on necessary work near the toll road. Others have suggested that the state could face difficulties if toll rates on the Indiana Toll Road begin to divert significant levels of traffic to surrounding roads. In such a case, the state could be constrained in making necessary improvements or constructing new facilities to handle the additional traffic. City of Chicago officials did not sign a noncompete provision in the Chicago Skyway contract. While city officials decided not to have a noncompete provision in order to keep their options open for future work they might find necessary, city officials told us that the concessionaire agreed to a lease agreement without such a provision because geographic limitations (the Chicago Skyway being located in a very heavily developed urban area and close to Lake Michigan) make construction of a competing facility very unlikely.

Spanish officials told us that they preserve flexibility by retaining the ability to renegotiate a concession agreement if it is in the public interest to do so. They referred to this as "rebalancing" a concession agreement. For example, if the government believes that adding capacity to a certain concession highway is in the public interest, it can require the concessionaire to do so as long as the government provides adequate compensation for the loss of revenues. Likewise, the government may rebalance a contract with a concessionaire if, for example, traffic is below forecasted levels, to help restore economic balance to the concession. In this case, the government might offer an extension to the concession term to allow the concessionaire more time to recover its investments. An executive of one concessionaire in Spain told us that it is important for the government to have that ability of renegotiation and concessionaires generally agree to the government's requests.

Workforce

Protection of the public interest has also extended to the workforce, and concession provisions have been used in this area as well. In some cases, public sector agencies entering into highway public-private partnerships with existing toll roads have contractually protected the interest of the existing toll road workforce by ensuring that workers are able to retain their jobs, or are offered employment elsewhere. Some public sector agencies have also addressed benefits issues. For example, in the Chicago Skyway concession there were 105 city employees when the concession began. According to the concession agreement, the city required the concessionaire to (1) comply with a living wage requirement;[34] (2) pay prevailing wages for all construction activities; and (3) make its best effort to interview (if requested), though not necessarily offer employment to, all Chicago Skyway employees for jobs before the asset was transferred. A Chicago official told us that once the concessionaire commenced operation five employees chose to maintain employment with the Chicago Skyway, while 100 took other city jobs.[35] Those employees that took other city jobs retained their previous benefits.

The state of Indiana also used concession provisions to help protect the workforce on the Indiana Toll Road. According to the concession agreement, these provisions required the concessionaire to follow certain laws such as nondiscrimination laws and minority-owned business requirements. Indiana officials told us that, prior to the lease agreement, the Governor of Indiana had made a commitment that each Indiana Toll Road employee would either be offered a job with the private concession company or with the state without a reduction in pay or benefits occurring with the new job. According to the Indiana DOT, all employees of the Indiana Toll Road (about 550 employees at the time the lease agreement commenced) were interviewed by the concessionaire; and about 85 percent of the employees transitioned to the private operator, but did so at equal or higher pay. According to an official with the toll road concessionaire, the average wages of an Indiana Toll Road employee increased from $11.00 per hour to between $13.55 and $16.00 per hour. Indiana officials indicated about 115 employees were offered placement with the state of Indiana and those that retained employment with merit or nonmerit state agencies maintained all outstanding vacation and sick time. Those toll road employees that left state agencies (including moving to the concessionaire) were paid for outstanding vacation time they had accrued, up to 225 hours. Indiana officials also indicated that, although those employees that left state agencies no longer are part of the state's pension plan, their contributions and their vested state contributions were preserved, and these employees are now offered a 401(k) plan by the concessionaire.

Another highway public-private partnership we examined, the TTC, involved new construction and, at the time of our review, had not yet reached the point of a concession. Oregon also involved new construction and was not at the point of a concession. Unlike existing facilities, new construction does not involve an existing workforce that could lose its jobs or face significantly different terms of work when the private sector takes over operations. However, concession terms can be used to protect the future workforce that is hired to construct and operate a highway built with a highway public-private partnership. For example, in a different highway public-private partnership project in Texas that has signed a concession, State Highway 130, segments 5 and 6, the concession agreement states that prevailing wage rates will be set by the Texas DOT and that the concessionaire should meet goals related to the hiring of women, minorities, and disadvantaged business enterprises. According to the Texas DOT, the concessionaire is also required to establish and implement a small business mentoring program.

Other countries have also acted to protect employees in highway public-private partnerships. For example, the United Kingdom has taken actions to ensure that the value gained in its highway public-private partnership projects is not done so at the expense of its workforce. According to the United Kingdom's Code of Practice on workforce matters, new and transferred employees of private concessionaires are to be offered "fair and reasonable" employment conditions, including membership in a pension plan which is at least equivalent to the public sector pension scheme that would apply. According to an official with the United Kingdom Treasury Department, this Code of Practice has been agreed to by both employers and trade unions and was implemented in 2003.

Oversight and Monitoring of Concessions

The public sector also undertakes oversight and monitoring of concessionaires to ensure that they fulfill their obligations to protect the public interest. Such mechanisms can both identify when requirements are not being met, and also provide evidence to seek remediation when the private sector does not do so. In Indiana, an Indiana Toll Road Oversight Board was created as an advisory board composed of both state employees and private citizens to review the performance and operations of the concessionaire and potentially identify cases of noncompliance. This Oversight Board meets on at least a quarterly basis and has discussed items dealing with traffic incidents, concerns raised by state residents and constituents, and the implementation of electronic tolling on the facility. The Chicago Skyway concession also incorporates oversight. Oversight includes reviewing various reports, such as financial statements and incident reports filed by the concessionaire, and hiring independent engineers to oversee the concessionaire's construction projects. In both Indiana and Chicago the concessionaire reimburses the public sector for oversight and monitoring costs— in Indiana up to $150,000 per year adjusted for inflation.

Oversight and monitoring also encompass penalties if a concessionaire breaches its obligations. For example, the highway public-private partnership contracts in Chicago and Indiana allow the public sector to ultimately regain control of the asset at no cost if the concessionaire is in material breach of contract. Additionally, the public sector has sometimes retained the ability to issue fines or citations to concessionaires for nonperformance. For example, according to the Texas DOT, in Texas an independent engineer will be assigned to the TTC concessionaire who will be able to issue "demerits" to the concessionaire for not meeting performance standards. These demerits, if not remedied, could lead to concessionaire default.

Foreign governments have also taken steps to provide oversight and monitoring of concessionaires. In Spain, the Ministry of Public Works assigns public engineers to each concession to monitor performance. These engineers not only monitor performance during construction to ensure that work is being done properly, but also monitor performance during operation. They do so by recording user complaints and incidents in which the concessionaire does not comply with the terms of the concession. Accountability and oversight mechanisms have also been incorporated in Australian concessions. In both Victoria and New South Wales, projects must demonstrate that they incorporate adequate information to the public on the obligations of the public and private sectors and that there are oversight mechanisms. In some instances, a separate statutory body, which may be chaired by a person outside of government, provides oversight, as was done on the CityLink toll road in Melbourne, Australia.[36] Officials with a private concessionaire in Australia told us that they generally meet monthly with the state Road and Traffic Authority to review concession performance. In addition, both the Victoria and New South Wales Auditor Generals are also involved with oversight. In both states the Auditor General reviews the contracts of approved highway public-private partnerships. In New South Wales, the law requires publication of these reviews and contract summaries. In Victoria, government policy requires publication of the contracts, together with project summaries, including information regarding public interest considerations.

Financial Analyses and Bidding Processes Have Also Been Used to Protect the Public Interest

Governments have also used financial analyses, such as asset valuations, and procurement processes to protect the public interest. We found that states and local governments entering into the two existing highway public-private partnerships that we reviewed largely limited their analyses to asset valuation. For example, both the city of Chicago and the state of Indiana hired consultants to value the Chicago Skyway and the Indiana Toll Road, respectively, before signing concessions for these assets. In Indiana, the state's consultant performed a net present valuation of the toll road that determined that the toll road was worth about $2 billion to the state. Because the winning bid of $3.85 billion that the state received was far more than the consultant's assessed value, Indiana used that valuation to justify that the transaction was in the public interest. The assistant budget director for Chicago told us that in Chicago an analysis showed the city could leverage only between $800 and $900 million from the toll road. The officials then compared that amount to the $1.8 billion that the city received from the winning bidder and determined that the concession was in the public interest. Both valuations assumed that future toll rates would increase only to a limited extent under public control.

Additionally, steps have been taken to protect the public interest through procurement processes. Both Chicago and Indiana used an auction bidding process in which qualified bidders were presented with the same contract and bid on the same terms. This process ensured that the winning bidder would be selected on price alone (the highest concession fee offered) since all other important factors and public interest considerations—such as performance standards and toll rate standards—would be the same for all bidders. Texas has also taken steps to protect the public interest through the procurement process for the TTC. While the Texas DOT signed the comprehensive development agreement with a private concessionaire for the TTC-35, it does not guarantee that the private firm will be awarded the concession for any segment of the TTC. All segments may be put out for competitive procurement; and, while the master development concessionaire has a right of first negotiation for some segments, it must negotiate with Texas and present a detailed facility plan. Additionally, according to the Texas DOT, the concessionaire is required to put together a facility implementation plan that, among other things, analyzes the projected budget and recommends a method for project delivery.

Foreign Governments Have Developed Public Interest Criteria and Assessment Tools

Some foreign governments have recognized the importance of public interest issues in public-private partnerships and have taken a systematic approach to these issues. This includes developing processes, procedures, and criteria for defining and assessing elements of the public interest and developing tools to evaluate the public interest of public-private partnerships. These tools include the use of qualitative public interest tests and criteria to consider when entering into public-private partnerships, as well as quantitative tests such as Value for Money (VfM) and PSCs, which are used to evaluate if entering into a project as a public-private partnership is the best procurement option available. According to a document from one state government in Australia (New South Wales), guidelines for private financing of infrastructure projects (which includes the development of public interest evaluation tools) supports the government's commitment to provide the best practicable level of public services by providing a consistent, efficient, transparent, and accountable set of processes and procedures to select, assess, and implement privately financed projects.

Some governments have laid out elements of the public interest in public-private partnerships and criteria for how those elements should be considered when entering into such agreements. These steps help ensure that major public interest issues are transparently considered in the public-private partnerships from the outset of the process, including highway public-private partnerships. For example, the state of Victoria in Australia requires all proposed public-private partnership projects to evaluate eight aspects of the public interest to determine how they would be affected.[37] These eight aspects include the following:

- *ffectiveness*. Whether the project is effective in meeting the government's objectives. Those objectives must be clearly determined.
- *Accountability and transparency*. Whether public-private partnership arrangements ensure that communities are informed about both public and private sector obligations and that there is oversight of projects.
- *Affected individuals and communities*. Whether those affected by public-private partnerships have been able to effectively contribute during the planning stages and whether their rights are protected through appeals and conflict resolution mechanisms.
- *Equity*. Whether disadvantaged groups can effectively use the infrastructure.
- *Public access*. Whether there are safeguards to ensure public access to essential infrastructure.
- *Consumer rights*. Whether projects provide safeguards for consumers, especially those for which the government has a high level of duty of care or are most vulnerable.
- *Safety and security*. Whether projects provide assurance that community health and safety will be secured.
- *Privacy*. Whether projects adequately protect users' rights to privacy.

Similarly, the government of New South Wales, Australia, also formally considers the public interest before entering into public-private partnerships. Public interest focuses on eight factors that are similar to Victoria's: effectiveness in meeting government objectives, VfM, community consultation, consumer rights, accountability and transparency, public access, health and safety, and privacy. The public interest evaluation is conducted up front prior to proceeding to the market and is updated frequently, including prior to the call for detailed proposals, after finalizing the evaluation of proposals, and prior to the government signing contract documents.

Additionally, foreign governments have also used quantitative tests to identify and evaluate the public interest and determine if entering into a project as a public-private partnership is the best option and delivers value to the public. In general, VfM evaluations examine total project costs and benefits and are used by some governments to determine if a public-private partnership approach is in the public interest for a given project. VfM tests are often done through a PSC, which compares the costs of doing a proposed public-private partnership project against the costs of doing that project through a public delivery model. VfM tests examine more than the financial value of a project and will examine factors that are hard to quantify, such as design quality and functionality, quality in construction, and the value of unquantifiable risks transferred to the private sector. VfM tests are commonly used in Australia, the United Kingdom, and British Columbia, Canada.

PSCs are often used as part of VfM tests. Generally speaking, a PSC test examines life-cycle project costs, including initial construction costs, maintenance and operation costs, and additional capital improvement costs that will be incurred over the course of the concession term. A PSC can also look at the value of various types of risk transfer to the private sector, whereby the more risk transferred to the private sector the more value to the public sector. For example, in the United Kingdom, use of the PSCs is mandated for all public-private partnership projects at both the national as well as local levels. British Columbia, Canada, also conducts a PSC for all public-private partnership proposals that compares the full life-cycle costs of procuring the proposed project as a public-private partnership, compared with a traditional design-bid-build approach. The British Columbia PSC not only compares the project costs but also evaluates the value of various risks. According to a Partnerships British Columbia official, the more risk transferred from the public to the private sector in a public-private partnership proposal, all else being equal, the better the value for the public. For example, this official said that the PSC they use will value a certain level of construction risk and determine the value (based on the costs and probability of that risk occurring) to the public sector of having the private sector assume that risk through a public-private partnership. The Partnerships British Columbia official also told us that the values of risks occurring are often not included in traditional public cost estimates, which is a reason that cost overruns are so common in public sector infrastructure projects. British Columbia uses the results of PSCs to help determine a project's procurement method. An official with British Columbia told us that many projects have been done through a traditional public procurement rather than privately because the results of the PSCs indicated that there was not enough value for money in the private approach.

Although PSCs can be helpful in identifying and evaluating the public interest, they have limitations. According to officials in Australia, Canada, and the United Kingdom, PSCs are composed of numerous assumptions, as well as projections years into the future. PSCs may have difficulty modeling long-term events and reliably estimating costs. Additionally, discount rates used in PSCs to calculate the present value of future streams of revenue may be arbitrarily chosen by the procuring authority if not mandated by the government. Officials with the Audit Office of New South Wales, Australia, raised similar concerns and said the volume and volatility of assumptions raise questions about the validity and accuracy of PSCs.[38] A government official with the U.K. told us that a limitation of its PSC is that it is a generic tool that applies to all privately financed projects, from transportation to hospitals, and therefore, there are some standard assumptions built into the model that may not be accurate for a transportation project. The official added that the government is considering working on creating a sector-specific PSC. However, despite these concerns there was general agreement among those with whom we talked that PSCs are useful tools.

While foreign governments may have extensive experience using PSCs and other public interest assessment tools, these tools continue to evolve based on experience and lessons learned. The use of formal tools and processes also does not guarantee that highway public-private partnerships will not face significant challenges and problems. For example, although a document we reviewed indicated that a formal assessment process and PSC was used to evaluate the Cross City Tunnel in Sydney, Australia, before it was built and operated through a concession agreement, this evaluation did not prevent the problems of low traffic, public opposition to the toll road, and bankruptcy that were discussed earlier in this chapter. The problems experienced led to changes in how public-private projects will be handled and evaluated in the future. According to the Director of the New South Wales Department of Treasury and Finance, one of the big lessons learned from the Cross City Tunnel experience was the importance of public outreach and communication. Documents from the New South Wales government also showed that public interest tools were strengthened. For example, in December 2006, the New South Wales guidelines for public-private partnerships were updated to, among other things, strengthen VfM tests by conducting them from the perspective of the user or taxpayer and requiring updates of the tests through the tender process. In addition, the New South Wales Department of Treasury and Finance issued new guidance on how to determine appropriate discount rates—an important component of PSCs. Evolution of tools has occurred in other countries as well. According to an official with British Columbia, the methodology of their PSC tests is reviewed by an independent auditor, and improvements to the methodology are continually made. Change in public interest evaluation tools has also occurred elsewhere. According to an official with the United Kingdom Treasury Department, after criticism about potential VfM benefits and the use of PSC models developed by consultants, the United Kingdom has moved from an advisor-driven PSC to a Treasury-driven two-part, four-stage VfM model that involves a simple spreadsheet and qualitative assessment. Even this new model is being considered for change due to complex contracting issues.

Use of Formal Public Interest Processes and Tools in the United States Are More Limited

We found a more limited use of systematic, formal processes and approaches to the identification and assessment of public interest issues in the United States. Both Oregon and Texas have used forms of PSCs. For example, Oregon hired a consultant to develop a PSC that compared the estimated costs of the private sector proposal for the Newburg-Dundee project with a model of the public sector's undertaking the project, using various public financing sources, including municipal debt and TIFIA loans. According to the Innovative Partnerships Project Director in the Oregon DOT, the results of this model were used to determine that the added costs of undertaking the project as a public-private partnership (given the need for a return on investment by the private investors) were not justifiable given the limited value of risk transfer in the project. While this PSC was conducted before the project was put out for official concession, the PSC was prepared after substantial early development work was done by private partners.

Similar to a PSC, Texas has developed "shadow bids" for two highway public-private partnerships in the state. These shadow bids included detailed estimates of design and construction costs, as well as operating costs and a detailed financial model, the results of which were compared against private sector proposals. While the model used by Texas is unique to each individual project, the methodology used (such as the estimation of future costs) is similar. In addition, the Director of the Texas Turnpike Authority of the Texas DOT told us that, while there are no statutory or regulatory provisions defining the public interest in public-private partnerships, when procuring public-private partnerships, the department develops specific evaluation procedures and criteria for that specific procurement, as well as contract provisions that are determined to be in the interests of the state. Public-private partnership proposals the department receives are then evaluated against those project criteria. However, these criteria are project-specific, and there are no standard criteria that are equally applied to all projects.

Neither Chicago nor Indiana had developed public interest tests or used PSCs prior to leasing of the Chicago Skyway or the Indiana Toll Road. Instead, analyses for these deals were largely focused on asset valuation and development of specific concession terms. Other state and local governments we spoke with said they have limited experience with using formal public interest criteria tools and tests. For example, the Chief Financial Officer of the California DOT told us that while the department is currently working with the California Transportation Commission to develop guidelines for public interest issues, this effort has not been finalized. Additionally, officials in New Jersey and Pennsylvania, two states that are exploring options, including private involvement, to better leverage existing toll roads, said that they have not yet created any formal public interest criteria or assessment tools such as PSCs. An official with the Illinois DOT also said that his state had not yet developed public interest criteria or assessment tools.

Not using formal public interest tests and tools means that aspects of the public interest can potentially be overlooked. For example, because VfM tests can allow the government to analyze the benefits and costs of doing a project as a public-private partnership, as opposed to other more traditional methods, not using such a test might mean that potential future toll revenues from public control of toll roads are not adequately considered. Neither Chicago nor Indiana gave serious consideration to the potential toll revenues they could earn by retaining control over their toll roads. In contrast, Harris County, Texas, in 2006 conducted a broad analysis of options for its public toll road system. This analysis was somewhat analogous to a VfM test. The analysis evaluated and conducted an asset valuation under three possible scenarios, including public control and a concession. This analysis was used by the county to conclude that it would gain little through a long-term concession and that through a more aggressive tolling approach, the county could retain control of the system and realize similar financial gains to those that might be realized through a concession.

Since public interest criteria and assessment tools generally mandate that certain aspects of the public interest are considered in public-private partnerships, if these criteria and tools are not used, then aspects of public interest might be overlooked. These aspects include such things as the following:

- *Transparency*. According to documents we reviewed, both Victoria and New South Wales, Australia, require transparency in public-private partnership projects so that communities and the public are well informed. Officials in Toronto, Canada, however, told us there was no such requirement and a lack of transparency about the 407 ETR concession—including information about the toll rate structure—meant that some people did not understand the objectives of the concession, as well as the tolling structure, and led to significant opposition to the project. The former Director of the Indiana Office of Management and Budget (OMB) told us that the Indiana legislature, as well as others, complained that the Indiana Toll Road lease was done in "secrecy."

- *Consideration of communities and affected interests.* Local and regional governments believe that there was limited coordination with them as well as the public on the TTC project. This lack of consideration of local and regional interests and concerns led to opposition by local and regional governments. That reaction helped drive statewide legislation that requires the state to involve local and regional governments to a greater extent in public-private partnerships. While Chicago considered the city's interests in the Chicago Skyway lease, it did not necessarily consider the interests of other parties, such as regional mobility. The Executive Director of the Chicago Metropolitan Agency for Planning (the metropolitan planning organization for the greater Chicago area) told us that regional interest issues, such as the traffic diversion onto local streets that might occur as a result of higher tolls on the Chicago Skyway, were not addressed in consideration of the lease. He added that, as a result, other routes near the Chicago Skyway might not be able to absorb the diverted traffic, causing regional mobility problems.

The use of formal public interest tests can also allow public agencies to evaluate the projected benefits, as well as the costs and trade-offs, of public-private partnerships. In addition, such tests can help determine whether or not the benefits outweigh the costs and if proceeding with the project as a partnership is the superior model, or if conducting the project through another type of procurement and financing model is better.

DIRECT FEDERAL INVOLVEMENT WITH HIGHWAY PUBLIC-PRIVATE PARTNERSHIPS HAS GENERALLY BEEN LIMITED, BUT IDENTIFICATION OF NATIONAL INTERESTS IN HIGHWAY PUBLIC-PRIVATE PARTNERSHIPS HAS BEEN LACKING

Direct federal involvement in highway public-private partnerships has generally been limited to projects in which federal requirements must be followed because federal funds have or will be used. While federal funding in highway public-private partnerships to date has been limited, the administration and DOT have actively promoted such partnerships through policies and practices, including developing experimental programs that waive certain federal regulations and encourage private investment. Although federal involvement with highway public-private partnerships is largely limited to situations where there is direct federal investment, recent highway public-private partnerships may, or could, have implications on national interests such as interstate commerce and homeland security. However, FHWA has given little consideration of potential national public interests in highway public-private partnerships. We have called for a fundamental reexamination of federal programs, including the highway program to identify specific national interests in the transportation system to help restructure existing programs to meet articulated goals and needs. This reexamination would provide an opportunity to define any national public interest in highway public-private partnerships and develop guidance for how such interests can best be protected. The increasing role of the private sector in financing and operating transportation infrastructure raises potential issues of national public interest. We also found that highway public-private partnerships that have, or will, use federal funds and involve tolling may be required by law to use excess toll revenues (revenues that are beyond that needed for debt service, a reasonable return on investment to a private party, and operation and maintenance) for projects eligible for federal transportation funding. However, the methodology for calculating excess toll revenues is not clear.

Direct Federal Involvement in Highway Public-Private Partnerships Has Generally Been Limited to Projects in which Federal Funds Have Been Invested

Direct federal involvement in highway public-private partnership projects is generally determined by whether or not federal funds were or will be involved in a highway project. As a result, FHWA has had a somewhat different involvement in each of the four U.S. highway public-private partnership projects we reviewed.

Indiana Toll Road

Since June 2006, the Indiana Toll Road has been operated by a private concessionaire under a 75-year lease. The Indiana Toll Road was constructed primarily with state funds and then incorporated into the Interstate Highway System. Although about $1.9 million in federal funds were used to build certain interchanges on the highway, Indiana subsequently repaid these funds. FHWA officials told us they did not review the lease of the highway to the private sector because there were no federal funds involved and no obligation on FHWA under title 23 of the U.S.C. to do so.

Chicago Skyway

The Chicago Skyway was leased in October 2004 to a private concessionaire. FHWA officials told us that they did not review the Chicago Skyway lease agreement before it was signed. Only a limited amount of federal funding was invested in the Chicago Skyway. According to FHWA, the state of Illinois received about $1 million in 1961 to construct an off-ramp from the Chicago Skyway to Interstate 94. In addition, about $14 million in federal funds were received in 1991 through an earmark in ISTEA. The Assistant Budget Director for Chicago told us the latter was for painting and various other improvements. FHWA officials stated that since the lease transaction did not involve any new expenditure of federal funds, there was no requirement that FHWA review and approve the lease before it was executed. According to FHWA officials, FHWA's primary role in the transaction was the modification of a 1961 toll agreement to allow Chicago to continue collecting tolls on the facility.

However, because federal funds were involved, FHWA did determine that two portions of federal law were applicable, one governing how proceeds from the lease of the asset—the up-front payment of $1.8 billion—were used and the other governing use of toll revenues.

- *Use of lease proceeds.* Proceeds from the lease of property acquired, even in part, with federal funds would be governed by section 156 of title 23 U.S.C. This section requires that states charge fair market value for the sale or lease of such assets and that the percentage of the income from the proceeds obtained from a sale or lease that represents the federal share of the initial investment (about $15 million in this case) be used by the state for title 23 eligible projects. Title 23 eligible projects can include construction of new transportation infrastructure. According to FHWA, the federal share in the Chicago Skyway ranged between 0.88 percent and 2.95 percent, depending on whether money from the ISTEA earmark was considered an addition to the real property or not and assuming control over the I-94 connector had been transferred to the contractor.[39] Title 23 of the U.S.C. covers a broad range of activities that are eligible for federal-aid highway funds, including reconstruction, restoration, rehabilitation, and resurfacing activities and the payment of debt service for a title 23 eligible project. FHWA determined that Chicago met its obligations under title 23 section 156 merely by retiring the Chicago Skyway debt ($392 million or nearly 25 percent of the lease proceeds).

* *Use of toll revenue.* When tolling is allowed on federally funded highways, the use of toll revenues is generally governed by section 129 of title 23 U.S.C. Under section 129, toll revenue must first be used for (1) debt service, (2) to provide a reasonable return on investment to any private party financing a project, and (3) the operations and maintenance of the toll facility. If there are any revenues in excess of these uses, and if the state or public authority certifies that the facility is adequately maintained, then the state or public authority may use any excess revenues for any title 23 eligible purpose. According to FHWA, since federal funds were expended in the Chicago Skyway, a toll agreement has been executed between FHWA, the Illinois DOT, city of Chicago, and Cook County providing that the toll revenues will be used in accordance with title 23 section 129.

Although FHWA determined that provisions governing excess toll revenues were met, it did not independently determine whether the rate of return to private investors would be reasonable. The rate of return is a critical component in determining whether excess revenues exist or not. According to FHWA officials there is no standard definition of what constitutes a "reasonable rate of return." Therefore, FHWA concluded it had no basis to evaluate the reasonableness of the return. In addition, FHWA officials stated that under guidance issued by the agency's Executive Director in 1995, the reasonableness of rate of return to a private investor is a matter to be determined by the state. FHWA officials said they relied on assurances from the city of Chicago that the rate of return was reasonable. According to DOT officials, FHWA determined that since the value of a concession was established through fair and open competitive procedures, the rate of return should be deemed to be reasonable. A review of the concession agreement indicates that the lease agreement was expected by the city of Chicago to "produce a reasonable return to the private operator" and that the city pledged "not to alter or revoke that determination" over the 99-year period of the lease. The Assistant Budget Director for Chicago also told us that the rates of return will be reasonable because a competitive bid process was used prior to signing a lease and that the concession agreement contains limitations of how much tolls can change over time—an important limitation since toll levels can significantly affect rates of return.

FHWA officials have recognized that concession arrangements governing facilities paid for largely with federal funds face a more difficult time meeting the requirements of sections 156 and 129 of title 23. For example, if a state received a $1 billion up-front payment to lease a highway built with 80 percent federal funds, the state would be required to invest $800 million of that payment in other title 23 eligible projects.

Trans-Texas Corridor

According to the Director of the Texas Turnpike Authority Division of the Texas DOT, Texas's intent is to make all transportation infrastructure projects eligible for federal aid whenever possible. While at the time of our review no federal funds had been expended on the Trans-Texas Corridor (TTC-35) project, Texas is considering using federal funds to complete parts of the corridor.

For the project to be eligible for federal funds, unless otherwise specified by FHWA, it must meet all federal requirements, including the environmental review process required under NEPA. The TTC-35 project is currently undergoing a two-tiered review process under NEPA. In Tier I, the Texas DOT has identified a potential 10-mile wide corridor through which the actual corridor will run, completed a draft environmental impact statement, which evaluates the impact of the project on the local and regional environment, and is awaiting federal approval through a record of decision. The record of decision, among other things, identifies the preferred alternative and provides information on the adopted means to avoid, minimize, and compensate for environmental impacts. The Tier I process is expected to be completed by early 2008. Tier II of the process will be used to determine the actual alignment of the road or rail line and will be completed in several parts for each facility, or unique segment of the facility. This process, like Tier I, includes identification of specific corridor segments, solicitation of public comments for each segment, and final approval, which will authorize construction. As we reported in 2003, environmental impact statements on federally funded highway projects take an average of 5 years to complete, according to FHWA.[40]

The state of Texas has also entered into a Special Experimental Project No. 15 (SEP-15)[41] agreement with FHWA for the TTC-35. According to FHWA, under this agreement FHWA has permitted the Texas DOT to release a request for proposals (RFP) and award the design-build contract prior to completion of the environmental review process. This sequence would not have been allowed under federal highway regulations existing at the time.[42] In accordance with the SEP-15 agreement, Texas entered into a contract with a private sector consortium to prepare a Master Development Plan for the TTC-35 and to assist in preparing environmental documents and analyses. The Master Development Plan is intended to help the state identify potential development options for the TTC-35 and to begin predevelopment work related to the project. The Master Development Plan also allows the private consortium to develop other highway facilities. In conjunction with this agreement, in March 2007, the private consortium was awarded a 50-year concession to construct, finance, operate and maintain State Highway 130, segments 5 and 6 (a highway that is expected to connect to the TTC-35).

Oregon

Similar to Texas, the Oregon Innovative Public-Private Partnerships Program is a program for the planning, acquisition, financing, development, design, construction, and operation of transportation projects in Oregon using the private sector as participants. Three projects have been identified under this program: (1) a potential widening of a 10-mile section of Interstate 205 (I-205) in the Portland area, (2) development of highways east of Portland serving existing industrial development and future residential and commercial development (called the Sunrise Corridor), and (3) construction of an 11-mile highway in the Newberg-Dundee corridor.

Oregon sought and received an FHWA SEP-15 approval for these projects. According to FHWA, the SEP-15 approval was to provide the Oregon DOT the flexibility to release an RFP and award a design-build contract prior to completion of the environmental review process, which was not permitted under federal highway regulations at the time. As discussed above, this requirement has changed. Subsequent to the SEP-15 approval, in October 2005, the state entered into an Early Development Agreement with FHWA that also permitted the state to engage the private sector in predevelopment activities prior to completion of the environmental review process. In January 2006, Oregon entered into preliminary development agreements with a private sector partner (Oregon Transportation Improvement Group) to proceed with predevelopment work on the three proposed projects. As of January 2007, Oregon had decided not to pursue the Sunrise Corridor project because it determined that projected toll revenue was not enough to cover the cost of operation or construction. Rather, Oregon plans to seek traditional funding sources. In July 2007, the state announced that it and the Oregon Transportation Improvement Group had ceased pursuing public-private development of the Newberg-Dundee project. According to the Oregon Department of Transportation, as of November 2007, the third project (I-205 lane widening) was not yet in the regional transportation plan but was expected to be added to the plan without difficulty. As of May 2007, federal funding ($20.9 million) had been used for such things as environmental assessment, planning, and right-of-way acquisition on the Newberg-Dundee project.

Federal Government Encourages and Promotes Highway Public-Private Partnerships through Policy and Practice

Although federal involvement with highway projects and highway public-private partnerships is largely governed by whether there is a direct federal investment in a project or not, the administration and DOT have actively encouraged and promoted the use of highway public-private partnerships. This effort has been accomplished through both policies and practices such as developing SEP-14 and SEP-15 procedures and preparing various publications and educational material on highway public-private partnerships.

Administration and DOT Actively Encourage and Promote Highway Public-Private Partnerships

Encouraging highway public-private partnerships is a federal governmentwide initiative articulated in the President's Management Agenda and implemented through the Office of Management and Budget (OMB). OMB promotes, among other things, increasing the level of competition from the private sector for services traditionally done by the public sector. DOT has followed this lead by incorporating highway public-private partnerships into its own policy statements. Its May 2006 *National Strategy to Reduce Congestion on America's Transportation Network* states that the federal government should "remove or reduce barriers to private investment in the construction or operation of transportation infrastructure."[43]

FHWA has used its administrative flexibility to develop three experimental programs to allow more private sector participation in federally funded highway projects. The first, SEP No. 14, or SEP-14, has been in place since 1990 to permit contracting techniques to be employed that deviate from the competitive bidding provisions of federal law required for any highway built with federal funds.[44] As those techniques have been approved for widespread use by FHWA since its enactment, the program has changed to allow other alternative contracting techniques, such as best value contractor selection[45] and the transfer of construction risk to the private construction contractor. States have used the techniques allowed under SEP-14 to allow more private sector involvement in building and maintaining transportation infrastructure than under traditional procurement methods. For example, states used design-build contracting[46] in almost 300 different construction and maintenance projects that were approved by FHWA between 1992 and 2003, including repavement of existing roads, bridge rehabilitation and replacement, and construction of additional highway lanes.

The second experimental program, the Innovative Finance Test and Evaluation Program (TE-045), was established in April 1994. This program was initially designed and subsequently operated to give states a forum in which to propose and test those concepts that best met their needs. Since TE-045 did not make any new money available, its primary focus was to foster the identification and implementation of new, flexible strategies to overcome fiscal, institutional, and administrative obstacles faced in funding transportation projects. States were encouraged to consider a number of areas in developing proposals under the program, including income generation possibilities for highway projects and alternative revenue sources, which could be pledged to repay highway debt. States were also encouraged to consider the use of federal-aid to promote highway public-private partnerships. According to FHWA, several types of financing tools were proposed by states and tested under TE-045. These included tools that provided expanded roles for the private sector in identifying and providing financing for projects, such as flexible matches and section 129 project loans.

The third experimental program, SEP No. 15, or SEP-15, is broad in scope and was designed to facilitate highway public-private partnerships and other types of innovation in the federal-aid highway process. SEP-15 allows for the modification of FHWA policy and procedure, where appropriate, in four different areas: contracting, compliance with environmental requirements, right-of-way acquisition, and project finance. According to FHWA, SEP-15 enables FHWA officials to review state transportation projects on a case-by-case basis to "increase project management flexibility, encourage innovation, improve timely project construction, and generate new revenue streams for federal-aid transportation projects."[47] While this program does not eliminate overall federal-aid highway requirements, it is designed to allow FHWA to develop procedures and approaches to reduce impediments to states' use of public-private partnerships in highway-related and other transportation projects. Table 6 summarizes the highway projects in which FHWA has granted SEP-15 approvals.

**Table 6. Highway Public-Private Partnerships with
SEP-15 Approval, as of June 2007**

Project	Date of SEP-15 approval	Description
TTC-35, Texas	February 2004	Proposed development of a new north-south highway, rail and public utilities corridor from the Mexican to Oklahoma borders in Texas.

Project	Date of SEP-15 approval	Description
Oregon Innovative Partnerships Program, Oregon	May 2005	An umbrella highway public-private partnership program under which three projects—South I-205 Corridor, Sunrise Project and Newberg-Dundee Transportation Improvement Project—have been identified for implementation.
Texas Toll Roads Statewide Open-Road Toll Collection System Project (Texas Toll Collection System), Texas	May 2005	Approval for contractor to design, build, operate, and maintain a statewide open-road tolling system.
Waiver of TIFIA requirements for several Texas DOT projects, Texas	February 2006	Approval for a private entity to develop, design, construct, finance, operate, maintain, and charge user fees for I-635 in the Dallas/Fort Worth metropolitan area, U.S. 281/Loop 1604 Toll Project in San Antonio, and the State Highway 161 project through Irving and Grand Prairie.
TTC-69, Texas	April 2006	Establishment of a new transportation corridor from northeast Texas to the United States-Mexico border, including tolled truck and car lanes, commuter, freight and high-speed passenger rail tracks, utilities and intermodal facilities.
Pocahontas Parkway, Virginia	August 2006	For the operation, maintenance, and toll collection for the existing Pocahontas Parkway and for the construction, maintenance, and operation of the new Richmond Airport Connector.
U.S. Highway 290, Texas	September 2006	Conversion of existing four-lane highway into a tolled highway with nontolled frontage roads in Travis County, Texas.
Connecting Idaho, Idaho	May 2007	Provision of Grant Anticipation Revenue Vehicle bonds to advance 260 miles of roadways located on 13 corridors in the state.
Knik Arm Crossing, Alaska	June 2007	Crossing links the municipality of Anchorage with the Matanuska-Susitna Borough.

Source: GAO analysis of FHWA data.

The SEP-15 flexibilities have been pivotal to allowing highway public-private partnership arrangements we reviewed in Texas and Oregon to go forward while remaining eligible for federal funds. For example, until August 2007, federal regulations did not allow private contractors to be involved in highway design-build contracts with a state department of transportation until after the federally mandated environmental review process under NEPA had been completed. The Texas DOT applied for a waiver of this regulation under SEP-15[48] for its TTC project to allow its private contractor to start drafting a comprehensive development plan to guide decisions about the future of the corridor before its federal environmental review was complete. FHWA approved this waiver, which allowed the contractor's work to proceed during the environmental review process and which could ultimately shorten the corridor's project time line. According to the Texas DOT, at all times, it and the FHWA maintain control over the NEPA decision-making process. The developer's role is similar to other stakeholders in the project. Similarly, Oregon used the SEP-15 process to experiment with the concept of contracting with a developer early in the project development phase for three potential projects in and around Portland, Oregon. Like Texas, Oregon wanted to involve the private sector prior to completion of the NEPA process.

FHWA and DOT Practices Also Promote Highway Public-Private Partnerships

FHWA and DOT have reinforced its legal and policy initiatives with promotional practices as well. These activities include the following:

- *Developing publications.* Publications include a public-private partnership manual that has material to educate state transportation officials about highway public-private partnerships and to promote their use. The manual includes sections on alternate federal financing options for highway maintenance and construction and outlines different federal legal requirements relating to highway public-private partnerships, including the environmental review process.[49] It also includes a public-private partnership user guide.[50] The user guide describes the many participants, stages of development, and factors (such as technical capabilities and project prioritization and selection criteria and processes) associated with developing and implementing public-private partnerships for transportation infrastructure projects.
- *Drafting model legislation for states to consider to enable highway public-private partnerships in their states.* The model legislation addresses such subjects as bidding, agreement structure, reversion of the facility to the state, remedies, bonds, federal funding, and property tax exemption, among other things.
- *Creating a public-private partnership Internet Web site.* This Web site serves as a clearinghouse of information to states and other transportation professionals about public-private partnerships, pertinent federal

regulations, and financing options.[51] It has links to FHWA's model public-private partnership legislation, summaries of selected highway public-private partnerships, key DOT policy statements, and the FHWA public-private partnership manual, among other things.

- *Making public presentations.* DOT and FHWA officials have made public speeches and written at least one letter to a state in support of highway public-private partnerships. For example, when Texas was considering modifying its public-private partnership statutes, FHWA's Chief Counsel, in a letter to the Texas DOT, warned that if Texas lost its initiative on highway public-private partnerships that "private funds flowing to Texas will now go elsewhere." DOT has also provided congressional testimony in support of highway public-private partnerships. For example, in a recent testimony to Congress, DOT's Assistant Secretary of Transportation for Policy stated that highway public-private partnerships are "one of the most important trends in transportation" and that DOT "has made expansion of public-private partnership[s] a key component" in DOT's on-going initiatives to reduce congestion and improve performance.[52]

- *Making tolling a key component of congestion mitigation.* Such a strategy could act to promote highway public-private partnerships since tolls provide a long-term revenue stream, key to attracting investors. One major part of DOT's May 2006 national strategy to address congestion is the Urban Partnership Agreement. Under the Urban Partnership Agreement, DOT and selected metropolitan areas will commit to aggressive strategies to address congestion. The key component of these aggressive strategies is tolling and congestion pricing. Congestion pricing could involve networks of priced lanes on existing highways, variable user fees on entire roadways, including toll roads and bridges, or area-wide pricing involving charges on all roads within a congested area.

National Interests in Highway Public-Private Partnerships Need to Be Identified

Although federal involvement with highway public-private partnerships is largely limited to situations where there is a direct federal investment, highway public-private partnerships can have implications on broader national interests, such as interstate commerce. FHWA officials told us that various federal laws and requirements that states must follow to receive federal funds are designed to protect national and public interests—for example, federally funded projects must receive environmental approval through the NEPA process. In addition, TIFIA loans must be investment grade and meet policy considerations they have some public interest criteria. However, FHWA officials told us that no specific federal definition of national public interest or federal guidance on identifying and evaluating national public interest exists. Thus, when federal funds are not involved in a project, there are few mechanisms to ensure that national public interests are identified, considered and protected. As a result, given the minimal federal funding in highway public-private partnerships we reviewed, little consideration has been given to potential national public interests in these partnerships.

Recent highway public-private partnerships have involved sizable investments of funds and significant facilities and suggest that implications for national public interests exist. For example, both the Chicago Skyway and the Indiana Toll Road are part of the Interstate Highway System; the Indiana Toll Road is part of the most direct highway route between Chicago and New York City and, according to one study, over 60 percent of its traffic is interstate in nature. However, federal officials had little involvement in reviewing the terms of either of these concession agreements before they were signed. In the case of Indiana, FHWA played no role in reviewing either the lease or national public interests associated with leasing the highway nor did it require the state of Indiana to review these interests. Similarly, development of the TTC may greatly facilitate North American Free Trade Agreement-related truck traffic nationwide. Although the TTC is going through the NEPA process, to date, no federal funding has been expended in the development of the project. In commenting on a draft of this chapter, DOT correctly noted that many of these same issues could be raised if the states involved had undertaken major projects with potential implications for national interests as publicly funded projects, using only state funds. Nevertheless, both state and DOT officials have also asserted that without a public-private partnership, these projects would not have advanced. In addition, public-private partnerships may present distinct challenges because they can and have involved long-term commitments of up to 99 years and the loss of direct public control—issues that are not present in state financed projects—and the fact that private entities are not accountable to the public in the same way public agencies are.

The absence of a clear definition of national public interests in the national transportation system is not unique to highway public-private partnerships. We have called for a fundamental reexamination of the federal role in highways and a clear definition of specific national interests in the system, including in such areas as freight mobility. A fundamental reexamination of federal surface transportation programs, including the highway program, presents the opportunity to address emerging needs, test the relevance of existing policies, and modernize programs for the twenty-first century. The growing role of the private sector in both financing and operating highway facilities raises the question of what role the private sector can and should play in the national transportation system and whether the presence of federal funding is the right criteria for federal involvement or whether other considerations should apply. For example, DOT has recognized the national importance of goods movement and the challenges of large, multimodal projects that cross state lines by establishing a "Corridors of the Future" program to encourage states to think beyond their boundaries in order to reduce congestion on some of the nation's most critical trade corridors. DOT plans to facilitate the development of these corridors by helping project sponsors reduce institutional and regulatory obstacles associated with multistate and multimodal corridor investments. Whether such corridors, which could be seen as being in the national interest, could be developed if portions of them were under effective private ownership is just one of many questions that could be addressed in identifying national public interests in general and public-private partnerships in particular. Once the national interest in highway public-private partnerships is more clearly defined, then an appropriate federal role in protecting and furthering those defined interests can be established.

The recent report by the National Surface Transportation Policy and Revenue Study Commission illustrates the challenges of identifying national public interests both in general and in public-private partnerships in particular. The report encouraged the use of public-private partnerships as an important part of financing and managing the surface transportation system as part of an overall strategy for aligning federal leadership and federal transportation investments with national interests. As discussed earlier, the commission recommended broadening states' flexibilities to use tolling and congestion pricing on the Interstate system but also recommended that that the public interest would best be served if Congress adopted strict criteria for approving public-private partnerships on the Interstate Highway System, including limiting allowable toll increases, prohibiting non-compete clauses, and requiring concessionaires to share revenues with the public sector. This definition of the public interest stands in sharp contrast to the dissenting views of three commissioners and to comments provided by DOT on a draft of this chapter. In their minority report, the dissenting commissioners stated that the Commission's recommendations would replace negotiated terms and conditions with a federal regulation and subject private toll operators to greater federal scrutiny than local public toll authorities. In commenting on a draft of this chapter, DOT stated that national interests are served by limiting federal involvement in order to allow these arrangements to grow and provide the benefits of which they are capable. These sharply divergent views should assist Congress as it considers the appropriate national interests and federal role in highway public-private partnerships.

CONCLUSIONS

Highway public-private partnerships show promise as a viable alternative, where appropriate, to help meet growing and costly transportation demands. The public sector can acquire new infrastructure or extract value from existing infrastructure while potentially sharing with the private sector the risks associated with designing, constructing, operating, and maintaining public infrastructure. However, highway public-private partnerships are not a panacea for meeting all transportation system demands, nor are they without potentially substantial costs and risks to the public—both financial and nonfinancial—and trade-offs must be made. While private investors can make billions of dollars available for critical infrastructure, these funds are largely a new source of borrowed funds, repaid by road users over what potentially could be a period of several generations. There is no "free" money in highway public-private partnerships.

Many forms of public-private partnerships exist both within and outside the transportation sector, and conclusions drawn about highway public-private partnerships—those involving long-term concession agreements—cannot necessarily be drawn about partnerships of other types and in other sectors. Highway public-private partnerships are fairly new in the United States, and although they are meant to serve the public interest, it is difficult to be confident that these interests are being protected when formal identification and consideration of public and national interests has been lacking, and where limited up-front analysis of public interest issues using established criteria has been conducted. Consideration of highway public-private partnerships could benefit from more consistent, rigorous, systematic, up-front analysis. Benefits are potential benefits—that is, they are not assured and can only be achieved by weighing them against potential costs and trade-offs through careful, comprehensive analysis to determine whether public-private partnerships are appropriate in specific circumstances and, if so, how best to implement them. Despite the need for careful analysis, the approach at the federal level has not been fully balanced, as DOT has done much to promote the benefits, but comparatively little to either assist states and localities weigh potential costs and trade-offs, nor to assess how potentially important national interests might be protected in highway public-private partnerships. This is in many respects a function of the design of the federal program as few mechanisms exist to identify potential national interests in cases where federal funds have not or will not be used. The historic test of the presence of federal funding may have been relevant at a time when the federal government played a larger role in financing highways but may no longer be relevant when there are new players and multiple sources of financing, including potentially significant private money. However, potential federal restrictions must be carefully crafted to avoid undermining the potential benefits, such as operational efficiencies, that can be achieved through the use of highway public-private partnerships. Reexamining the federal role in highways provides an opportunity to identify the emerging national public interests, including the national public interests in highway public-private partnerships.

Finally, in the future, states may seek increased federal funding for highway public-private partnerships or seek to monetize additional assets for which federal funds have been used. If this occurs, then it is likely some portion of toll revenues may need to be used for projects that are eligible for federal transportation funding. Clarifying the methodology for determining excess toll revenues and reasonable rates of return in highway public-private partnerships, would give clearer guidance to states and localities undertaking highway public-private partnerships and help reduce potential uncertainties to the private sector and the financial markets.

MATTER FOR CONGRESSIONAL CONSIDERATION

A reexamination of federal transportation programs provides an opportunity to determine how highway public-private partnerships fit in with national programs as well as an opportunity to identify the national interests associated with highway public-private partnerships. In order to balance the potential benefits of highway public-private partnerships with protecting key national interests, Congress should consider directing the Secretary of Transportation to consult with them and other stakeholders to develop and submit objective criteria for identifying national public interests in highway public-private partnerships. In developing these criteria, the Secretary should identify any additional legal authority, guidance, or assessment tools required, as appropriate and needed, to ensure national public interests are protected in future highway public-private partnerships. The criteria should be crafted to allow the department to play a targeted role in ensuring that national interests are considered in highway public-private partnerships, as appropriate.

RECOMMENDATION FOR EXECUTIVE ACTION

To ensure that future highway public-private partnerships meet federal requirements concerning the use of excess revenues for federally eligible transportation purposes, we recommend that the Secretary of Transportation direct the Federal Highway Administrator to clarify federal-aid highway regulations on the methodology for determining excess toll revenue, including the reasonable rate of return to private investors in highway public-private partnerships that involve federal investment.

AGENCY COMMENTS AND OUR EVALUATION

We provided copies of the draft chapter to DOT for comment prior to finalizing the chapter. DOT provided its comments in a meeting with the Assistant Secretary for Transportation Policy and the Deputy Assistant Secretary for Transportation Policy on November 30, 2007. DOT raised substantive concerns with several of the draft chapter's findings and conclusions, as well as one of the recommendations. Specifically, DOT commented that the draft chapter did not analyze the benefits of highway public-private partnerships in the context of current policy and traditional procurement approaches. DOT stated that highway public-private partnerships are a potentially powerful response to current and emerging policy failures in the federal-aid highway program that both DOT and GAO have identified over the years. For example, DOT asserted that the current federal-aid program (1) encourages the misallocation of resources, (2) does not promote the proper pricing of transportation assets, including the costs of congestion, (3) is not tied to achieving defined results and (4) provides weak incentives for innovation. DOT also stated that—in addition to supplying large amounts of additional capital to improve U.S. transportation infrastructure—public-private partnerships are responsive to a crisis of performance in government stewardship of the transportation network and traditional procurement approaches. DOT noted that highway public-private partnerships can bring discipline to the decision-making process, result in more efficient use of resources, and produce lower capital and operating costs, resulting in lower total costs of projects than under traditional public procurement approaches. DOT stated that traditional procurement approaches produce comparatively inferior results.

We agree with DOT that highway public-private partnerships have the potential to provide many benefits and that a number of performance problems characterize the current federal-aid highway program. Our draft chapter discusses the potential benefits cited by DOT, although we revised our draft chapter to better clarify the potential benefits of pricing and resource efficiencies of highway public-private partnerships that DOT cited in its comments. However, we also believe that all the benefits DOT cited are *potential* benefits—they are not assured and can be achieved only through careful, comprehensive analysis to determine whether public-private partnerships are appropriate in specific circumstances and, if so, how best to structure them. Among the benefits that DOT cited was the ability of highway public-private partnerships to supply additional capital to improve transportation infrastructure. As our chapter states, this capital is not free money but is rather a form of privately issued debt that must be repaid to private investors seeking a return on their investment by collecting toll revenues. Regarding DOT's comment about policy failures in the federal-aid highway program, we believe the most direct strategy to address performance issues is to reexamine and restructure the program considering such factors as national interests in the transportation system and specific performance-related goals and outcomes related to mobility. Such a restructuring would help (1) better align and allocate resources, (2) promote proper pricing, (3) achieve defined results, and (4) provide incentives for innovation. We believe our chapter places highway public-private partnerships in their proper context as viable potential alternatives that must be considered in such a reexamination and, therefore, made no further changes to the chapter.

Regarding DOT's characterization of a crisis of performance in government stewardship of the transportation network and assertion that the traditional procurement approaches produce comparatively inferior results, our past work has recognized concerns about particular projects and public agencies, as well as improvements that are needed to public procurement processes in general. It was not within the scope of our review to systematically compare the results of projects acquired through public-private partnerships with those acquired through traditional procurement approaches. Nevertheless, we believe neither our work— nor work by others—provides a foundation sufficient to support DOT's sweeping characterization of public stewardship as a "crisis," or its far-reaching conclusion that traditional procurement approaches produce inferior results compared with public-private partnerships. We, therefore, made no further changes to our chapter.

DOT also disagreed with much of our discussion concerning protection of the public interest in highway public-private partnerships. DOT stated that many federal and state laws govern how transportation projects are selected and delivered, including highway public-private partnerships, and that the draft chapter did not explain why highway projects delivered through public-private partnerships pose additional challenges to protecting the public interest, or why there should be a greater interest in such projects than in highways built and operated by state and local governments. In response to DOT's comments, we added additional information to the final chapter about initiatives that certain states have taken to identify and protect the public interest in highway public-private partnerships. We agree that federal and state laws governing traditional highway procurement contain mechanisms to protect the public interest and that many of the public interest concerns are the same regardless of how the project is delivered. However, we continue to believe that additional and more systematic approaches are necessary with highway public-private partnerships given the long-term nature of concession agreements (up to 99 years in some cases), the potential loss of public control, and the fact that private entities are not accountable to the public in the same way public agencies are.

Similarly, DOT disagreed with our discussion of national public interests and stated that our draft chapter did not explain why highway projects undertaken through highway public-private partnerships raise issues of potential national interests more so than if a state or local government undertook them. DOT stated that the chapter did not adequately explain how highway public-private partnerships impact national interests, such as interstate commerce, that would allow policy makers to clearly understand the nature of those concerns and assess what actions are needed to address them. As stated above, we agree that highway projects delivered through state and local governments raise many of the same concerns but that additional and more systematic approaches are necessary with highway public-private partnerships. Furthermore, it was not the objective of our chapter to define what the national interest concerns were on particular projects or to suggest what actions were needed to address such concerns. Rather, our chapter illustrates that such projects may have implications for national interests, and that it is important to consider such interests and their implications up-front as part of the decision-making process in order to ensure that any potential concerns are identified, evaluated, and resolved. At the current time, there is little mechanism to allow such consideration when federal funds are not involved with a project. As discussed in our chapter, the reexamination of federal transportation programs, which we have called for in previous chapters, provides an opportunity to determine the most appropriate structure of these federal programs, where highway public-private partnerships fit into this structure, and the identification of national interests associated with highway public-private partnerships.

Finally, DOT indicated that the scope of our work focused primarily on a subset of public-private partnerships involving long-term concession agreements and, as a result, our conclusions cannot be generalized to other types of public-private partnerships. We agree with DOT that the scope of our work only focused on a subset of all types of public-private partnerships. Our chapter acknowledges that there are also public-private partnerships in nontransportation areas, as well as in other modes of transportation (such as mass transit). We also acknowledge that there are other types of highway public-private partnerships, such as availability payments, that are not included in our scope. In response to DOT's comments, we made these scope limitations clearer in our chapter and acknowledged that the findings and conclusions of our chapter cannot necessarily be extrapolated to other types of public-private partnerships.

Our draft chapter recommended that DOT develop and submit to Congress a legislative proposal that establishes objective criteria for identifying national public interests in highway public-private partnerships, including any additional legal authority required by the Secretary of Transportation necessary to develop regulations, guidance, and assessment tools, as appropriate, to ensure such interests are protected in future highway public-private partnerships. DOT disagreed with this recommendation, stating that the draft chapter did not provide sufficient evidence to explain why the federal government should intrude on inherently state activities or to justify a more expansive federal role. Instead, DOT stated that federal involvement should be limited in order to allow these arrangements to grow and provide the benefits of which they are capable. As discussed in our chapter, the reexamination of federal transportation programs provides an opportunity to determine the most appropriate structure of these federal programs, where highway public-private partnerships fit into this structure, and the identification of potential national interests that are associated with highway public-private partnerships. We believe that once these specific national interests have been established, instead of necessarily leading to a more expansive federal role, the federal government can play a more targeted role—including ensuring that identified national interests in highway public-private partnerships are considered by states and localities, as appropriate. We have, therefore, deleted our recommendation but have instead suggested that Congress consider directing DOT to undertake these actions.

We also recommended that the Secretary of Transportation direct the Administrator of FHWA to clarify federal-aid highway regulations on the methodology for determining excess toll revenue, including a reasonable rate of return to private investors in highway public-private partnerships. DOT indicated, in response to this recommendation, that it would reexamine the regulations and take appropriate action, as necessary, to ensure the regulations are clear. Therefore, we made no change to the recommendation.

DOT also provided technical comments that were incorporated, as appropriate. We also obtained comments from states, localities, and organizations in the foreign countries included in our review. In general, these comments were technical in nature and were incorporated where appropriate.

Congressional Requesters

The Honorable James M. Inhofe
Ranking Member
Committee on Environment and Public Works
United States Senate

The Honorable Peter A. DeFazio
Chairman Subcommittee on Highways and Transit
Committee on Transportation and Infrastructure
House of Representatives

The Honorable Richard J. Durbin
United States Senate

APPENDIX I: SCOPE AND METHODOLOGY

Our work was focused on federal surface transportation and highway programs and the issues associated with use of private sector participation in providing public transportation infrastructure. In particular, we focused on (1) the benefits, costs, and trade-offs associated with highway public-private partnerships; (2) how public officials have identified, evaluated, and acted to protect the public interest in public-private partnership arrangements; and (3) the federal role in highway public-private partnerships and potential changes needed in this role. Our scope was limited to identifying the primary issues associated with using public-private partnerships for highway infrastructure and not in conducting a detailed financial analysis of the benefits and costs of specific arrangements. We selected recent projects to review, such as the lease of the Chicago Skyway and the Indiana Toll Road and planning for the Oregon and Trans-Texas Corridor (TTC), to understand decision-making processes. These projects were selected because they were recent examples of highway public-private partnerships, were large dollar projects, or used different approaches to highway public-private partnerships. We also spoke with states that were considering highway public-private partnerships, including California, New Jersey, and Pennsylvania.

It was not our intent to review all highway public-private partnerships in the United States. We also did not review all types of highway public-private partnerships. For example, we did not review highway public-private partnerships involving shadow tolling or availability payments. In shadow tolling, the public sector pays a private sector company an amount per user of a roadway as opposed to direct collection of a toll by the private company. In availability payments, a private company is paid based on the availability of a highway to users. These were not included in our scope and the findings and conclusions of this study cannot necessarily be extrapolated to those or other types of public-private partnerships. In reviewing highway public-private partnerships, it was not our intent to either endorse or refute these projects but rather to identify key public policy issues associated with using public-private partnerships to provide highway infrastructure.

To identify the benefits, costs, and trade-offs associated with public-private partnerships for tolled highway projects, we collected and reviewed relevant documents including concession agreements, planning documents, toll schedules, guidance, and academic, corporate, and government chapters. We obtained toll schedule data from the Chicago Skyway concession company and used them to project a range of future maximum toll rates using.Congressional Budget Office estimates of future growth rates for gross domestic product (GDP) and the consumer price index (CPI) and Census Bureau forecasts for population growth (in order to determine forecasted per capita GDP). We also conducted interviews with public-sector representatives from state departments of transportation; elected officials; public-interest groups; municipal planning organizations; Federal Highway Administration (FHWA) representatives; and other representatives at municipal, state, and federal levels. We also spoke with foreign government representatives in the United Kingdom, and we visited relevant public- and private-sector representatives in Canada, Spain, and Australia to understand the foreign perspective and to identify common benefits, costs, and trade-offs experienced in other countries. The countries we visited to obtain information on highway public-private partnerships was based on those countries that had a history of using highway public-private partnerships to obtain highway infrastructure, had highway public-private partnerships in place for a period of time so lessons learned could be determined, or had developed tools to assess public interest issues. These foreign public-private partnership experiences were compared with experiences in the United States. We conducted interviews with the private-sector concessionaires, financial investors, and legal, technical and financial advisors to the public and private sectors. Finally, we visited public-private partnership projects, including the Chicago Skyway, the Indiana Toll Road, and the 407 Express Toll Road (ETR) in Toronto, Canada.

To assess the reliability of the Chicago Skyway historic toll data, we (1) reviewed sources containing historic toll information, including the city's request for qualifications from potential concession companies, an academic paper, and a relevant journal article and (2) worked closely with the Assistant Budget Director for the city of Chicago to identify any data problems. We found a discrepancy in the toll rates and brought it to the official's attention and worked with him to determine the correct historic toll rates. We determined that the data were sufficiently reliable for the purposes of this chapter. To estimate each year's population in order to estimate annual GDP per capita, we used the Census Bureau's interim population projections, which were created in 2004, and which project population growth in 10-year increments. We computed the average annual rate of increase in estimated population for every 10-year period and then used each 10-year period's annual average rate of increase to estimate the population for each year in that period. As a base population estimate, we used the Census Bureau's population estimate of just over 303 million on January 1, 2008. We divided the forecasted nominal GDP for every year by the projected population in that year to determine the forecasted per capita nominal GDP. We determined the Census Bureau data were reliable for use by checking for obvious errors or omissions, as well as anomalies such as unusual data points. We used the CPI to convert past and projected toll rates to 2007 dollars. To convert amounts denominated in foreign currencies, we converted to 2007 U.S. dollars using the Organization for Economic Cooperation and Development's purchasing power parities for GDPs. To obtain information on the value of concession agreements and the use of lease proceeds, we obtained financial information from the concession companies and state representatives.

To determine how public officials have identified, evaluated, and acted to protect the public interest in public-private partnership arrangements, we conducted site visits of highway public-private partnerships and visited selected foreign countries with long-term experience of conducting highway public-private partnerships. We visited the state of Oregon to examine three potential public-private partnership projects in the metropolitan Portland region. We also conducted site visits for the Chicago Skyway and Indiana Toll Road, as well as the TTC in Texas, and the 407 ETR in Toronto, Canada. We also conducted visits to Spain, the states of New South Wales, and Victoria in Australia. For each site visit, we met with relevant officials from public sector agencies, such as state departments of transportation and state financial agencies, consultants and advisors to the public sector, including legal, financial, and technical advisors; the private sector operators; and other relevant stakeholders, such as users groups. Interviews covered a wide range of topics, including a discussion of how the public interest was defined, evaluated and protected in the relevant public-private partnership project. In addition to conducting interviews, we collected relevant documents, including legal contracts, public interest assessment tool guidance, procurement documents, financial statements, and reports, and analyzed them as necessary. Where appropriate, we reviewed contracts for certain public interest mechanisms. In addition to those site and country visits, we met with officials from British Columbia, Canada, and the United Kingdom to discuss their processes and tools for evaluating and protecting the public interest. We also held interviews with officials of FHWA and collected and analyzed policy and legal documents related to public interest issues.

To address the federal role in highway public-private partnerships, we reviewed pertinent legislation; prior GAO reports and testimonies; and other documents from FHWA, state department of transportation (DOT), and foreign national and provincial governments. This included policy documents from DOT, the public-private partnership Internet Web site developed by FHWA, model legislation prepared by FHWA, the FHWA public-private partnership manual, and various public presentations made by FHWA officials about highway public-private partnerships issues. We also obtained data from FHWA on the use of the SEP-14 and SEP-15 processes, including a list of projects approved to use these processes. Further, we obtained data from FHWA on the use of private activity bonds in the context of highway-related projects. After checking for obvious errors or omissions, we deemed these data reliable for our use. We discussed federal tax issues, including deduction from income of depreciation for highway public-private partnerships, with both FHWA and a tax expert associated with the Chicago Skyway lease. Our discussion of national interests in highway projects was based on a review of DOT's fiscal years 2006 to 2011 strategic plan, documentation of the Department of Defense Strategic Highway Network, and pertinent legislation related to the National Highway System. We also interviewed FHWA officials, officials from state DOTs and local governments, officials from private investment firms, and officials from foreign national and provincial governments that have entered into highway and other public-private partnerships. Discussions with FHWA included clarifying how it determines such things as reasonable rates of return on highway projects where there is private investment and the use of proceeds when there is federal investment in a highway facility that is leased to the private sector. Where feasible, we corroborated these clarifications with documents obtained from FHWA.

We conducted this performance audit from June 2006 to February 2008 in accordance with generally accepted government auditing standards. Those standards require that we plan and perform the audit to obtain sufficient, appropriate evidence to provide a reasonable basis for our findings and conclusions based on our audit objectives. We believe that the evidence obtained provides a reasonable basis for our findings and conclusions based on our audit objectives.

APPENDIX II: PROFILE OF GAO PUBLIC-PRIVATE PARTNERSHIP CASE STUDIES

Case Study: Chicago Skyway, Chicago, Illinois

Project description: The Chicago Skyway is a 7.8-mile elevated toll road connecting Interstate 94 (Dan Ryan Expressway) in Chicago to Interstate 90 (Indiana Toll Road) at the Indiana border. Built in 1958, the Skyway was operated and maintained by the city of Chicago Department of Streets and Sanitation. In March 2004, the city of Chicago issued a request for qualifications from potential bidders interested in operating the facility on a long-term lease basis. It received 10 responses and in May 2004 invited five groups to prepare proposals. Bids were submitted in October 2004, with the long-term concession awarded to the Skyway Concession Company (SCC) that included Cintra and Macquarie on October 27, 2004. This was the date the contract was signed.

Project concession fee: Cintra/Macquarie bid $1.83 billion.

Concession term: 99 years.

Institutional arrangements: Cintra is a part of Grupo Ferrovial, one of the largest infrastructure development companies in Europe and Macquarie Infrastructure Group, a subsidiary of Macquarie Bank Limited, Australia's largest investment bank. SCC assumed operations on the Chicago Skyway on January 24, 2005. SCC is responsible for all operating and maintenance costs of the Chicago Skyway but has the right to all toll and concession revenue. This agreement between SCC and the project sponsor, city of Chicago, was the first long-term lease of an existing public toll road in the United States.

Financing: Original financial structure was: Cintra equity—$485 million; Macquarie equity—$397 million; and bank loans—$1 billion (approximately). SCC subsequently refinanced the capital structure in 2005, which reduced the equity holdings of Cintra and Macquarie to approximately $500 million. Originally financed by European banks, the $1.550 billion refinancing also included Citgroup. The refinancing involved capital accretion bonds ($961 million) with a 21-year maturity with an interest rate equivalent to 5.6 percent. There is an additional $439 million in 12-year floating rate notes, and $150 million in subordinated bank debt provided by Banco Bilbao Vizcaya Argentaria and Santander Central Hispano of Spain, together with Calyon of Chicago.[1]

Revenue sources: Based on tolls: up to $2.50 until 2008; $3.00 until 2011, $3.50 until 2013, $4.00 until 2015, $4.50 until 2017, $5.00 starting in 2017.

Lease proceeds: Proceeds from the agreement paid off $463 million of existing Chicago Skyway debt; $392 million to refund long- and short-term debt and to pay other city of Chicago obligations; $500 million for long-term and $375 million for a medium-term reserve for the city of Chicago, as well as a $100 million neighborhood, human, and business infrastructure fund to be drawn down over 5 years.

Case Study: Indiana Toll Road, Northern Indiana

Project description: The Indiana Toll Road stretches 157 miles across the northernmost part of Indiana from its border with Ohio to the Illinois state line, where it provides the primary connection to the Chicago Skyway and downtown Chicago. The Indiana Toll Road links the largest cities on the Great Lakes with the Eastern Seaboard, and its connections with Interstate 65 and Interstate 69 lead to major destinations in the South and on the Gulf Coast. For the past 25 years, the Indiana Toll Road has been operated by the Indiana DOT. In 2005, the Governor of Indiana tasked the Indiana Finance Authority to explore the feasibility of leasing the toll road to a private entity. A *Request for Toll Road Concessionaire Proposals* was published on September 28, 2005. Eleven teams submitted proposals by the October 26 deadline. The lease concession was awarded to Indiana Toll Road Concession Company LLC (ITRCC) comprised of an even public-private partnership between Cintra and Macquarie.

Project concession fee: ITRCC submitted the highest bid of $3.8 billion.

Concession term: 75 years.

Institutional arrangements: ITRCC is composed of a 50/50 public-private partnership between Cintra, which is part of Grupo Ferrovial, and Macquarie

Infrastructure Group. The Indiana Toll Road lease transaction was contingent upon authorizing legislation. House Enrolled Act 1008, popularly known as "Major Moves," was signed into law in mid-March 2006. On April 12, 2006, the Indiana Toll Road and the Indiana Finance Authority executed the "Indiana Toll Road Concession and Lease Agreement." Pursuant to its terms, the Indiana Finance Authority agreed to terminate the current operational lease to the Indiana DOT. A 10-member board of directors oversees ITRCC and its operations of the Indiana Toll Road. ITRCC formally assumed operational responsibility for the toll road on June 29, 2006.

Financing: The financing structure is Cintra Equity—$385 million; Macquarie Equity—$385 million; and bank loans—$3.030 billion. Loans were provided by a collection of seven European banks: (1) Banco Bilbao Vizcaya Argentaria SA; (2) Banco Santander Central Hispano SA; and (3) Caja de Ahorros y Monte de Piedad de Madrid, all of Spain; BNP Paribas of France; DEPFA Bank of Germany; RBS Securities Corporation of Scotland, and Dexia Crédit Local, a Belgian-French bank.

Revenues: Based on tolls: $8.00 through June 30, 2010, for two-axle vehicles with higher tolls for three- to seven-axle vehicles. From June 30, 2011, tolls can be based on 2 percent or the percentage increase of the CPI or per capita nominal GDP whichever is greater.

Lease proceeds: The concession fee will provide funding for the Major Moves program, which will support about 200 new construction and 200 major preservation projects around the state, including beginning construction of Interstate 69 between Evansville and Indianapolis. The proceeds will also fund projects in the seven toll road counties and provide $150 million over 2 years to all the state's 92 counties for roads and bridges.

Case Study: Trans-Texas Corridor, Texas

Project description: The TTC program is envisioned to be a 4,000-mile network consisting of a series of interconnected corridors containing tolled highways for automobile traffic and separate tolled truckways for motor carrier traffic; freight, intercity passenger, and commuter rail lines; and various utility rights-of-way. The Texas Transportation Commission formally adopted a TTC action plan in June 2002, which identified four priority segments of the TTC, which roughly parallel the following existing routes: Interstate 35 from Oklahoma to San Antonio and Interstate 37 from San Antonio south to the border of Mexico; Interstate 69 from Texarkana to Houston to Laredo and the lower Rio Grande

Valley; Interstate 45 from Dallas-Fort Worth to Houston; and Interstate 10 from El Paso in the west, to the border of Louisiana at Orange. Plans call for the TTC to be completed over the next 50 years with routes prioritized according to Texas' transportation needs. Texas DOT, the state transportation agency, will oversee planning, construction, and ongoing maintenance although private vendors can deliver the services including daily operations.

In 2005, the Texas DOT selected a consortium led by Cintra and Zachry Construction Corporation under a competitively procured comprehensive development agreement (CDA) to develop preliminary concept and financing plans for TTC-35, including segments comprising the 600-mile Interstate 35 corridor in Texas. Included in this plan are facilities adjacent to Interstate 35 between Dallas and San Antonio consisting of a four-lane toll road that could eventually include separate truck toll facilities, utilities, and freight, commuter, and high-speed rail lines. Under the terms of the CDA, Cintra-Zachry produced the master development and financial plan for TTC-35. Once the master plan is complete, individual project segments—be they road, rail, utilities, or a combination of these—may be developed, as specified in the separate facility implementation plans as part of the master plan. Cintra-Zachry will have the right of first negotiation for development of some facilities developed in the master plan subject to Texas DOT's approval. According to the Texas DOT, the contract only required the department to negotiate in good faith for possible concession contracts valuing at least $400 million. The award of the State Highway 130, segment 5 and 6 agreement discussed above fully meets the requirements of the CDA. However, Cintra-Zachry is eligible for consideration on future TTC-35 facilities.

Project cost: Initial cost estimates for the full 4,000 mile TTC project range from $145 billion to $184 billion in 2002 dollars, as reported in the Texas DOT's June 2002 TTC Plan. According to the Texas DOT, this would include all highway and rail modes fully built as envisioned in the 2002 plan. The Texas DOT acknowledges that many of the proposed facilities or modes may not be needed. Implementation of this plan includes the flexibility to build only what will be needed.

Institutional arrangements: The consortium Cintra-Zachry, LP is 85 percent owned by Cintra Concesiones de Infraestructuras de Transporte, S.A. and 15 percent owned by Zachry Construction Corporation. Zachry Construction Corporation is a privately owned construction and industrial maintenance service company located in San Antonio, Texas. The Cintra-Zachry team produced the master development plan and financial plan for TTC-35. This plan was accepted by the Texas DOT in 2006. The team may opt to perform additional activities such as financing, planning, design, construction, maintenance, and toll collection and operation of segments of the approved development plan for the corridor, as approved by the Texas DOT and FHWA.

Project financing: To be determined for entire TTC program. The final Cintra-Zachry TTC-35 proposal called for a capital investment of $6 billion in a tollroad linking Dallas and San Antonio, and $1.2 billion in concession payments to Texas DOT for the right to operate the facility for 50 years. According to the Texas DOT, the current Master Development Plan shows approximately $8.8 billion and $2 billion, respectively.

Revenue sources: Tolls. The CDA between Cintra-Zachry and Texas DOT does not specify how toll rates will be set and adjusted or the term of any toll concessions for the corridor. According to the Texas DOT, state statute and department policy require the Texas DOT to approve all rate setting and rate escalating methodologies. The CDA requires Cintra-Zachry to be compliant with these regulations. The State Highway 130 agreement specifically sets toll rates and the formula for future adjustments.

Lease proceeds: To be determined.

Case Study: Oregon

Project descriptions: In January 2006, the Oregon Transportation Commission approved the Oregon DOT agreements with the Oregon Transportation Improvement Group (OTIG) for predevelopment work on three proposed public-private partnership highway projects—Sunrise Corridor, South Interstate 205 Widening, and Newberg-Dundee Transportation Improvement Projects. The proposed Sunrise Corridor is construction of a new four-lane, limited access roadway facility to SE 172nd (segment 1) and additional transportation infrastructure to serve the newly incorporated city of Damascus (segment 2). The proposed South Interstate 205 Corridor Improvements project is a widening of this major north-south freight and commuter route in the Portland metropolitan region. The proposed Newberg-Dundee project is an identified alternative corridor (bypass) that is approximately 11 miles long, starting at the east end of Newberg and ending near Dayton at the junction with Oregon 18.

Under an agreement with Macquarie, Macquarie will do the predevelopment work for all three projects as three separate contracts and will internalize the predevelopment costs for each project if that project proceeds into implementation. If the project does not proceed, then Oregon DOT will reimburse Macquarie for the predevelopment work for that project.

Project updates:

Sunrise corridor: OTIG and Oregon DOT determined that the Sunrise Corridor would not be toll-viable, and decided to indefinitely postpone the project. This decision was based on the project not offering substantial time savings to other alternative routes in the area and the predictability of traffic on the proposed project was uncertain. According to an Oregon DOT official, the project will be put on hold and may be reconsidered in the future, but it is not considered a priority at this time. Oregon DOT paid Macquarie $500,000 for the study.

South Interstate 205 widening: According to an Oregon DOT official, this project is not yet listed in the regional transportation plan but the environmental review process has already begun. Final decisions on whether this project will proceed will not occur until the environmental assessment is completed.

Newberg-Dundee: In July 2007, OTIG and Oregon DOT agreed to cease pursuing public-private development of a Newberg-Dundee tolled bypass after an independent analysis confirmed that the plan to charge a toll on the bypass alone would not produce sufficient revenue to finance the planned project under a public-private concession agreement. Instead, according to an Oregon DOT official, the project will likely be continued under a traditional public sector procurement approach using the private sector as contractors. According to this official, the road is still expected to be tolled.

Case Study: Highway 407 ETR, Toronto, Canada

Project description: Highway 407 ETR stretches 108 kilometers through the Greater Toronto Area. In 1998, as part of the largest privatization project in Canadian history at that time, the Province of Ontario put out a tender for the operation of the original 68 kilometers of highway and the requirement to build the remaining 40 kilometers. Following an international competition, the 407 ETR consortium led by Cintra of Grupo Ferrovial, SNC-Lavalin and Capital D'Amerique CDPQ was awarded the 99-year contract in 1999.

Project cost: $3.1 billion Canadian dollars for a 99-year lease.

Institutional arrangements: The 407 ETR consortium was initially led by Cintra of Grupo Ferrovial, SNC-Lavalin and Capital D'Amerique CDPQ. In 2002, Macquarie Infrastructure Group purchased all of Capital D'Amerique CDPG's interest in the toll road.

Revenue sources: Tolls are based on level of traffic flow. Toll rates are guaranteed to increase at 2 percent per year for the first 15 years and by an amount set by the concessionaire if traffic exceeds certain traffic levels.

Lease proceeds: Most of the proceeds were deposited into a general consolidated revenue fund and each resident of Ontario received a $200 check from the government for the sale.

REFERENCES

[89] GAO, *Performance and Accountability: Transportation Challenges Facing Congress and the Department of Transportation*, GAO-07-545T (Washington, D.C.: Mar. 6, 2007). The Highway Trust Fund is made up of two accounts, the Highway Account and the Mass Transit Account. In fiscal year 2005, the Highway Trust Fund had total receipts of about $37.9 billion of which the Highway Account represented $32.9 billion and the Mass Transit Account about $5.0 billion.

[90] GAO-07-545T.

[91] GAO, Highlights of a Forum Convened by the Comptroller General of the United States: Transforming Transportation Policy for the 21st Century, GAO-07-1210SP (Washington, D.C.: Sept. 19, 2007).

[92] American Association of State Highway and Transportation Officials, Transportation - Invest in Our Future: Future Needs of the U.S. Surface Transportation System (February 2007).

[93] For example, FHWA views "design-build" contracting, under which a single contractor designs and constructs a facility under the same contract, as a public-private partnership.

[94] National Surface Transportation Policy and Revenue Study Commission, *Report of the National Surface Transportation Policy and Revenue Study Commission, Transportation for Tomorrow*, December 2007. This commission was created under SAFETEA-LU.

[95] Qualified PABs are tax-exempt bonds issued by a state or local government, the proceeds of which are used for a defined qualified purpose by an entity other than the government that issued the bond.

[96] See GAO, Federal-Aid Highways: Increased Reliance on Contractors Can Pose Oversight Challenges for Federal and State Officials, GAO-08-198 (Washington, D.C.: Jan. 8, 2008), for more information about contracting of highway work.

[97] U.S. Department of Transportation, Federal Highway Administration, *Synthesis of Public-Private Partnership Projects for Roads, Bridges and Tunnels From Around the World–1985-2004*, Aug. 30, 2005. This report was prepared by AECOM Consult Team. According to FHWA, the data used for this report was based on information developed and maintained by the editor of *Public Works Financing*, a periodical that provides information and views regarding financing issues, trends, methods, and projects involving public-use infrastructure, and should be considered approximate.

[98] GAO, Highways and Transit: Private Sector Sponsorship of and Investment in Major Projects Has Been Limited, GAO-04-419 (Washington, D.C.: Mar. 25, 2004).

[99] As of April 2007.

[100] Spain did not pursue new public-private partnerships during the period 1985 to 1995 because the government in power during that period pursued toll-free roads instead.

[101] This amount has been converted to U.S. dollars from Canadian dollars using the Organization for Economic Cooperation and Development's purchasing power parities for gross domestic products.

[102] GAO, Transportation Infrastructure: Cost and Oversight Issues on Major Highway and Bridge Projects, GAO-02-702T (Washington, D.C.: May 1, 2002); GAO, Federal-Aid Highways: FHWA Needs a Comprehensive Approach to Improving Project Oversight, GAO-05-173 (Washington, D.C.: Jan. 31, 2005).

[103] Seventy-four percent of highway projects met the goal in 2004; 79 percent met the goal in 2005; and 82 percent met the goal in 2006.

[104] U.S. Department of Transportation, *Report to Congress on Public-Private Partnerships* (December 2004).

[105] However, profits are not always guaranteed and bankruptcies have resulted, as discussed earlier.

[106] According to the Chief Executive Officer of the Chicago Skyway, "concession rights" is treated as an Internal Revenue Code section 197 intangible and is amortized in 15 years, regardless of the lease term or the useful life of the asset. However, costs allocated to "tangible assets" are subject to the normal depreciation rules. This official also told us that about $1.5 billion of the Chicago Skyway lease amount was for concession rights, and $334 million was allocated to the tangible asset.

[107] Depreciation is the accounting process of allocating against revenue the cost expiration of tangible property, plant, and equipment. Under

straight-line depreciation, an equal amount of depreciation expense is taken annually over the life of the asset. Under accelerated depreciation, a depreciation expense is taken that is higher than annual straight-line amount in the early years and lower in later years.

[108] Prior to the passage of SAFETEA-LU in 2005, only public agencies could issue federal tax-exempt bonds.

[109] FHWA has approved another private activity bond for $1.866 billion for SH-121 in Texas. However, Texas is currently awarding that contract to the North Texas Toll Authority, a public toll authority, which has stated that it will not use private activity bonds for this project.

[110] This official also told us that the refinancing occurred to reduce the initial equity investment in the project (which was nearly 50 percent) and increase the debt investment. Investment officials told us that typically private investment in highway public-private partnerships is 40 percent equity and 60 percent debt.

[111] GAO, Highway Finance: States' Expanding Use of Tolling Illustrates Diverse Challenges and Strategies, GAO-06-554 (Washington, D.C.: June 28, 2006).

[112] According to FHWA officials, some states have dealt with toll equity and income levels with various assistance packages for low-income users.

[113] In Chicago, tolls are subject to scheduled increases until 2017 and, in Indiana, until mid-2010.

[114] Potential future tolls on the Chicago Skyway in this analysis were limited to a 40-year horizon due to the unreliability of GDP projections beyond this time period. See appendix I for further information on toll projections used for this analysis.

[115] As discussed earlier, under terms of the concession agreement and estimated increases in nominal GDP, our analysis shows that tolls on the Chicago Skyway will be permitted to increase in real terms nearly 97 percent (about 1.7 percent annually) from 2007 to 2047. In nominal terms, this is a total increase of nearly 397 percent (or about an average annual increase of just over 4 percent).

[116] GAO-04-419.

[117] According to DOT officials, these projects were financed through models different than the public-private partnerships that are the focus of this report.

[118] The Chief Financial Officer of the California DOT noted that the cost of buying back the road was still below what it would have cost the public sector to build it and that the road has proven to be a valuable asset.

[119] The Texas DOT noted that the moratorium included a number of exceptions.

[120] As discussed earlier in this report, refinancing may occur early in a concession period as the initial investors either attempt to "cash out" their investment—that is, sell their investment to others and use the proceeds for other investment opportunities—or obtain new, lower cost financing for the existing investment. Refinancing may also be used to reduce the initial equity investment in public-private partnerships.

[121] As discussed earlier, the Orange County Transportation Authority purchased the rights to operate the SR-91 managed lanes so it would no longer be constrained by the noncomplete clause preventing it from conducting needed work on the adjacent untolled publicly operated lanes.

[122] A living wage is a wage that is above federal or state minimum wage requirements and is considered the wage needed for a full-time worker to support a family at some level above the federal poverty line.

[123] According to the Skyway Concession Company, none of the five employees stayed with the concessionaire.

[124] The Melbourne City Link Authority was initially responsible for oversight of the CityLink toll road. This organization was ultimately absorbed into VicRoads, the public agency responsible for all of Victoria's roads.

[125] For more information, see *Public-Private Partnerships Victoria, Information Brochure, Government of Victoria, www.vic.gov.au/treasury* (undated).

[126] An official with the New South Wales Department of Treasury stated that New South Wales has a well-established methodology for determining discount rates, which is based on the Capital Asset Pricing Model. In addition, in February 2007, the New South Wales government released a technical paper to assist in the determination of appropriate discount rates in evaluating private financing proposals for public sector projects.

[127] According to a concessionaire official, the connector ramp from the Chicago Skyway to Interstate 94 was not transferred as part of the lease.

[128] GAO, Highway Infrastructure: Stakeholders' Views on Time to Conduct Environmental Reviews of Highway Projects, GAO-03-534 (Washington, D.C.: May 23, 2003).

[129] Under SEP-15, FHWA allows a waiver of certain federal regulations to permit private sector involvement in projects prior to completion of the environmental review process. A more detailed discussion of SEP-15 can be found later in this report.

[130] FHWA officials told us that, since the FHWA's SEP-15 approval of this project, Congress enacted section 1503 of SAFETEA-LU requiring FHWA to revise its design-build regulations to permit the release of an RFP and the award of a design-build contract prior to the completion of the environmental review process. On August 14, 2007, the FHWA published a final rule implementing the new regulations.

[131] U.S. Department of Transportation, National Strategy to Reduce Congestion on America's Transportation Network (May 2006).

[132] These alternative techniques include cost-plus-time bidding, lane rental, design-build contracting, and warranty clauses.

[133] In best value contracting, the selection of a contractor is based on a combined technical score and price.

[134] In design-build contracting, the contracting agency specifies the end result, and the design criteria and the prospective offerors submit proposals based on their selection of design, materials, and construction methods. The design-build contracting approach results in one award for both the design and construction of a project, thus eliminating the need for a separate bidding process for the construction phase.

[135] DOT, FHWA, Manual, p. 36.

[136] Texas originally applied under SEP-14 but was transferred by FHWA to the SEP-15 program.

[137] Federal Highway Administration, Department of Transportation, Manual for Using Public-Private Partnerships on Highway Projects.

[138] U.S. Department of Transportation, Federal Highway Administration, Office of Policy and Governmental Affairs, prepared by AECOM Consult Team, User Guidebook on Implementing Public-Private Partnerships for Transportation Infrastructure Projects in the United States, Final Report Work Order 05-002 (July 7, 2007).

[139] This Web site can be found at http://www.fhwa.dot.gov/ppp/.

[140] Statement of Tyler Duvall, Assistant Secretary of Transportation for Policy, U.S. Department of Transportation, Before the Committee on

Transportation and Infrastructure, Subcommittee on Highways and Transit, U.S. House of Representatives, February 13, 2007.

Appendix II

[141] According to the SCC, some of the interest rates are based on the London Interbank Overnight Rate plus various percentages.

In: Public-Private Partnerships
Editor: Leslie R. Kellerman, pp. 131-144
ISBN: 978-1-60692-358-0
© 2009 Nova Science Publishers, Inc.

Chapter 3

HIGHWAY PUBLIC-PRIVATE PARTNERSHIPS: SECURING POTENTIAL BENEFITS AND PROTECTING THE PUBLIC INTEREST COULD RESULT FROM MORE RIGOROUS UP-FRONT ANALYSIS[*]

JayEtta Z. Hecker

July 24, 2008
Mr. Chairman and Members of the Subcommittee:

We appreciate the opportunity to testify on public-private partnerships and their role in the surface transportation system. As you know, America's transportation system is the essential element that facilitates the movement of both people and freight within the country. Nevertheless, the current federal approach to addressing the nation's surface transportation problems is not working well. Despite large increases in expenditures in real terms for transportation, the investment has not commensurately improved the performance of the nation's surface transportation system, as congestion continues to grow and looming problems from the anticipated growth in travel demand are not being adequately addressed. We have called for a fundamental reexamination of our surface transportation policies, including creating well-defined goals based on identified

---

[*] Excerpted from GAO Report GAO-08-1052T, dated July 24, 2008.

areas of national interest, incorporating performance and accountability into
funding decisions, and more clearly defining the role of the federal government as
well as the roles of state and local governments, regional entities, and the private
sector.

The private sector has long been involved in surface transportation as
contractors in the design and construction of highways. In recent years, the private
sector has become increasingly involved in assuming other responsibilities
including planning, designing, and financing. Under some of these arrangements,
the private sector is being looked to not only to construct facilities, but also to
finance, maintain, and operate facilities under long-term concession agreements—
up to 99 years in one case. In some cases, this involves financing and constructing
a new facility and then operating and maintaining it over a specified period of
time. In other cases, this involves operating and maintaining an existing toll road
for a period of time in exchange for an up-front payment provided to the public
sector and the right to collect tolls over the term of the agreement.

We recently issued a report on public-private partnerships in the highway
sector. For this hearing, you asked us to discuss this report—in particular, the
financing and tax issues it raised. My remarks today are based on this February
2008 report[1] and focus on (1) the benefits, costs, and trade-offs to the public
sector associated with highway public-private partnerships; (2) how public
officials have identified and acted to protect the public interest in highway public-
private partnerships; and (3) the federal role in highway public-private
partnerships and potential changes in this role. We performed our work in
accordance with generally accepted government auditing standards. Those
standards require that we plan and perform the audit to obtain sufficient,
appropriate evidence to provide a reasonable basis for our findings and
conclusions based on our audit objectives. We believe that the evidence obtained
provides a reasonable basis for our findings and conclusions based on our audit
objectives.

We limited the term "highway public-private partnerships" to highway-
related projects in which the public sector enters into a contract, lease, or
concession agreement with a private sector firm or firms, and where the private
sector provides transportation services such as designing, constructing, operating,
and maintaining the facility, usually for an extended period of time. This
definition included long-term concessions for toll roads in which the private
sector firm(s) receives some or all toll revenues over the life of the lease or
concession agreement with the public sector. There are numerous other types of
arrangements classified as "public-private partnerships" that we did not include.
For example, we did not include fee-for-service arrangements in which effective

ownership of a transportation facility does not transfer to the private sector. We also recognize that there may be other forms of highway public-private partnerships. We did not include these types of public-private partnerships in the scope of our work, and the findings and conclusions of our work cannot be extrapolated to those or other types of public-private partnerships.

In summary:

- Highway public-private partnerships have resulted in advantages for state and local governments, such as obtaining new facilities and value from existing facilities without using public funding. The public can potentially obtain other benefits, such as sharing risks with the private sector, more efficient operations and management of facilities, and, through the use of tolling, increased mobility and more cost-effective investment decisions. There are also potential costs and trade-offs. There is no "free" money in public-private partnerships. They are potentially more costly to the public and it is likely that tolls on a privately operated highway will increase to a greater extent than they would on a publicly operated toll road. There is also the risk of tolls being set that exceed the costs of the facility, including a reasonable rate of return, should a private concessionaire gain market power because of the lack of viable travel alternatives. There are also financial trade-offs. Unlike public toll authorities, the private sector pays federal income taxes and can deduct depreciation on assets for which they have effective ownership for tax purposes. The extent of these deductions and the amount of the foregone revenue, if any, to the federal government is difficult to determine. Obtaining these deductions may also require lengthy concession periods. According to experts involved in the lease of the Chicago Skyway and the Indiana Toll Road, demonstrating effective ownership contributed to the 99-year and 75-year concession terms for the two facilities, respectively. Financial experts also told us that in the absence of the depreciation benefit, the concession payments to Chicago and Indiana would likely have been less than the $1.8 billion and $3.8 billion, respectively.
- Highway public-private partnerships in the U.S. we have reviewed sought to protect the public interest largely through concession agreement terms prescribing performance and other standards. While these protections are important, governments in other countries, including Australia and the United Kingdom, have developed systematic approaches to identifying and evaluating public interest before agreements are entered into,

including the use of public interest criteria, as well as assessment tools, and require their use when considering private investments in public infrastructure. For example, a state government in Australia uses a public interest test to determine how the public interest would be affected in eight specific areas, including whether the views and rights of affected communities have been heard and protected and whether the process is sufficiently transparent. While similar tools have been used to some extent in the United States, their use has been more limited. Using up-front public interest analysis tools can also assist public agencies in determining the expected benefits and costs of a project and an appropriate means to deliver the project. Not using such tools may lead to certain aspects of protecting the public interest being overlooked.

- Direct federal involvement in highway public-private partnerships has generally been limited to projects in which federal requirements must be followed because federal funds have or will be used. While direct federal involvement has been limited, the Department of Transportation (DOT) has done much to promote highway public-private partnerships, but comparatively little to either assist states and localities in weighing potential costs and trade-offs, or to assess how potentially important national interests might be protected in such arrangements. Given the minimal federal funding in highway public-private partnerships to date, little consideration has been given to potential national public interests in them. Highway public-private partnerships may pose national public interest implications such as interstate commerce that transcend whether there is direct federal investment in a project. The historic test of the presence of federal funding may have been relevant at a time when the federal government played a larger role in financing highways but may no longer be relevant when there are new players and multiple sources of financing, including potentially significant private money. We have called for a fundamental reexamination of federal programs to address emerging needs and test the relevance of existing policies. Such a reexamination provides an opportunity to identify emerging national public interests (including tax considerations), the role of highway public-private partnerships in supporting and furthering those national interests, and how best to identify and protect national public interests in future public-private partnerships. We believe DOT has the opportunity to play a targeted role in ensuring that national interests are considered, as appropriate, and have suggested that Congress consider directing the Secretary of Transportation to develop and submit objective criteria for identifying national public interests in highway public-private partnerships, including any additional legal authority, guidance, or assessment tools that would be appropriately required. We recognize this is no easy task—any potential federal restrictions on highway public-private partnerships must be carefully crafted to avoid undermining the potential benefits that can be achieved.

HIGHWAY PUBLIC-PRIVATE PARTNERSHIPS CAN POTENTIALLY PROVIDE BENEFITS BUT ALSO ENTAIL COSTS, RISKS, AND TRADE-OFFS

Highway public-private partnerships have the potential to provide numerous benefits to the public sector. There are also potential costs and trade-offs.

Potential Benefits

Highway public-private partnerships created to date have resulted in advantages from the perspective of state and local governments, such as the construction of new infrastructure without using public funding and obtaining funds by extracting value from existing facilities for reinvestment in transportation and other public programs. For example, the state of Indiana received $3.8 billion from leasing the Indiana Toll Road and used those proceeds to fund a 10-year statewide transportation plan. As we reported in 2004, by relying on private-sector sponsorship and investment to build roads rather than financing the construction themselves, states (1) conserve funding from their highway capital improvement programs for other projects, (2) avoid the up-front costs of borrowing needed to bridge the gap until toll collections became sufficient to pay for the cost of building the roads and paying the interest on the borrowed funds, and (3) avoid the legislative or administrative limits that govern the amount of outstanding debt these states are allowed to have.[2] All of these results are advantages for the states.

Highway public-private partnerships potentially provide other benefits, including the transfer or sharing of project risks to the private sector. Such risks include those associated with construction costs and schedules and having sufficient levels of traffic and revenues to be financially viable. Various government officials told us that because the private sector more reliably analyzes its costs, revenues, and risks throughout the life cycle of a project and adheres to scheduled toll increases, it is able to accept large amounts of risk at the outset of a project, although the private sector prices all project risks and bases its final bid proposal, in part, on the level of risk involved. In addition, the public sector can potentially benefit from increased efficiencies in operations and life-cycle management, such as increased use of innovative technologies.

Highway public-private partnerships can also potentially provide mobility and other benefits to the public sector, through the use of tolling. The highway public-private partnerships we reviewed all involved toll roads. These benefits include better pricing of infrastructure to reflect the true costs of operating and maintaining the facility and thus improved condition and performance of public infrastructure, as well as the potential for more cost effective investment decisions by private investors. In addition, through congestion pricing, tolls can be set to vary during congested periods to maintain a predetermined level of service, creating incentives for drivers to consider costs when making their driving decisions, and potentially reducing the demand for roads during peak hours.

Potential Costs, Risks, and Trade-offs

Although highway public-private partnerships can be used to obtain financing for highway infrastructure without the use of public sector funding, there is no "free money" in highway public-private partnerships.

Rather, this funding is a form of privately issued debt that must be repaid. Private concessionaires primarily make a return on their investment by collecting toll revenues. Though concession agreements can limit the extent to which a concessionaire can raise tolls, it is likely that tolls will increase on a privately operated highway to a greater extent than they would on a publicly run toll road. Tolls are generally set in accordance with concession agreements and, in contrast to public-sector practices, allowable toll increases can be frequent and automatic. The public sector may lose control over its ability to influence toll rates, and there is also the risk of tolls being set that exceed the costs of the facility, including a reasonable rate of return if, for example, a private concessionaire gains market power because of the lack of viable travel alternatives. In addition, highway public-private partnerships also potentially require additional costs to the public sector compared with traditional public procurement, including the costs associated with (1) required financial and legal advisors, and (2) private-sector financing compared with public-sector financing.

In addition to potentially higher tolls, the public sector may give up more than it receives in a concession payment in using a highway public-private partnership with a focus on extracting value from an existing facility. In exchange for an up-front concession payment, the public sector gives up control over a future stream of toll revenues over an extended period of time, such as 75 or 99 years. It is possible that the net present value of the future stream of toll revenues (less operating and capital costs) given up can be much larger than the concession payment received. Concession payments could potentially be less than they could or should be. Conversely, because the private sector takes on substantial risks, the opposite could also be true—that is, the public sector might gain more than it gives up.

Using a highway public-private partnership to extract value from an existing facility also raises issues about the use of those proceeds and whether future users might potentially pay higher tolls to support current benefits. In some instances, up-front payments have been used for immediate needs, and it remains to be seen whether these uses provide long-term benefits to future generations who will potentially be paying progressively higher toll rates to the private sector throughout the length of a concession agreement. Both Chicago and Indiana used their lease fees, in part, to fund immediate financial needs. Both also established long-term reserves from the lease proceeds. Conversely, proceeds from the lease of Highway 407 ETR in Toronto, Canada, went into the province's general revenue fund.

Financial Trade-offs

Trade-offs from the public perspective can also be financial, as highway public-private partnerships have implications for federal tax policy. Private firms generally do not realize profits in the first 10 to 15 years of a concession agreement. However, the private sector receives benefits from highway public-private partnerships over the term of a concession in the form of a return on its investment. Private-sector investors generally finance large public-sector benefits early in a concession period, including up-front payments for leases of existing projects or capital outlays for the construction of new, large-scale transportation projects. In return, the private sector expects to recover any and all up-front costs, as well as ongoing maintenance and operation costs, and generate a return on investment. Furthermore, any cost savings or operational efficiencies the private sector can generate, such as introducing electronic tolling, improving maintenance practices, or increasing customer satisfaction in other ways, can further boost the return on investment through increased traffic flow and increased toll revenue.

Unlike public toll authorities, private-sector firms pay federal income tax. Current tax law allows private sector firms to deduct depreciation on assets involved with highway public-private partnerships for which they have "effective ownership." Effective ownership of assets requires, among other things, that the length of a concession agreement be equal to or greater than the useful economic life of the asset. According to financial and legal experts, including those who were involved in the lease of the Chicago Skyway in Chicago, Illinois, and the Indiana Toll Road, the useful economic life of those facilities was lengthy. The requirement to demonstrate effective asset ownership thus required lengthy partnership concession periods and contributed to the 99-year and 75-year concession terms for the Chicago Skyway and Indiana Toll Road, respectively. These financial and legal experts told us that as effective owners, the private investors can claim full tax deductions for asset depreciation within the first 15 years of the lease agreements.[3]

Determining the extent of depreciation deductions associated with highway public-private partnerships, and the extent of foregone revenue to the federal government, if any, from these deductions is difficult to determine because they depend on such factors as taxable income, total deductions, and marginal tax rates of private-sector entities involved with highway public-private partnerships. Financial experts told us that in the absence of the depreciation benefit, the concession payments to Chicago and Indiana would likely have been less than the $1.8 billion and $3.8 billion paid, respectively.

However, foregone revenue to the federal government from tax benefits associated with transportation projects can potentially amount to millions of dollars.[4] For example, as we reported in 2004, foregone tax revenue when the private-sector used tax-exempt bonds to finance three projects with private sector involvement—the Pocahontas Parkway, Southern Connector, and Las Vegas Monorail—were between $25 million and $35 million.[5]

HIGHWAY PUBLIC-PRIVATE PARTNERSHIPS HAVE SOUGHT TO PROTECT PUBLIC INTEREST IN MANY WAYS, BUT USE OF PUBLIC INTEREST CRITERIA IS MIXED IN THE UNITED STATES

The public interest in highway public-private partnerships can and has been considered and protected in many ways. State and local officials in the U.S. projects we reviewed heavily relied on concession terms. Most often, these terms were focused on, among other things, ensuring performance of the asset, dealing with financial issues, and maintaining the public sector's accountability and flexibility. Included in the protections we found in agreements we reviewed were:

- Operating and maintenance standards: These standards are put in place to ensure that the performance of the asset is upheld to high safety, maintenance, and operational standards and can be expanded when necessary. For example, based on documents we reviewed, the standards on the Indiana Toll Road require the concessionaire to maintain the road's condition, utility, and level of safety including a wide range of roadway issues, such as signage, use of safety features such as barrier walls, snow and ice removal, and the level of pavement smoothness that must be maintained.
- Expansion trigger requirements: These triggers require that a concessionaire expand a facility once congestion reaches a certain level. Some agreements can be based on forecasts. For example, on the Indiana Toll Road, when service is forecasted to fall below certain levels within 7 years, the concessionaire must act to improve service, such as by adding additional capacity at its own cost.
- Revenue-sharing mechanisms: These mechanisms require a concessionaire to share some level of revenues with the public sector. For example, on one Texas project, if the annual return on investment of the private concessionaire is at or below 11 percent, then the state could share in 5 percent of all revenues. If it is over 15 percent, the state could receive as much as 50 percent of the net revenues.

While these protections are important, governments in other countries, including Australia and the United Kingdom, have developed systematic approaches to identifying and evaluating public interest before agreements are entered into, including the use of public interest criteria, as well as assessment tools, and require their use when considering private investments in public infrastructure. These tools include the use of qualitative public interest tests and criteria to consider when entering into public-private partnerships. For example, a state government in Australia uses a public interest test to determine how the public interest would be affected in eight specific areas, including whether the views and rights of affected communities have been heard and protected and whether the process is sufficiently transparent. These tools also include quantitative tests such as Value for Money and public sector comparators, which are used to evaluate if entering into a project as a public-private partnership is the best procurement option available.

While similar tools have been used to some extent in the United States, their use has been more limited. For example, Oregon hired a consultant to develop public-sector comparators to compare the estimated costs of a proposed highway public-private partnership with a model of the public sector's undertaking the project. According to the Innovative Partnerships Project Director in the Oregon DOT, the results of this model were used to determine that the added costs of undertaking the project as a public-private partnership (given the need for a return on investment by the private investors) were not justifiable given the limited value of risk transfer in the project. While this study was conducted before the project was put out for official concession, it was prepared after substantial early development work was done by private partners. Neither Chicago nor Indiana had developed public interest tests or other tools prior to the leasing of the Chicago Skyway or the Indiana Toll Road.

Using up-front public interest analysis tools can assist public agencies in determining the expected benefits and costs of a project and an appropriate means to undertake the project. Not using such tools may lead to certain aspects of protecting public interest being overlooked. For example, concerns by local and regional governments in Texas helped drive statewide legislation requiring the state to involve local and regional governments to a greater extent in future highway public-private partnerships. Elsewhere, in Toronto, Canada, the lack of a transparency about the toll rate structure and misunderstanding about the toll structure of the Highway 407 ETR facility was a major factor in significant opposition to the project.

DIRECT FEDERAL INVOLVEMENT WITH HIGHWAY PUBLIC-PRIVATE PARTNERSHIPS HAS GENERALLY BEEN LIMITED, BUT IDENTIFICATION OF NATIONAL INTERESTS IN HIGHWAY PUBLIC-PRIVATE PARTNERSHIPS HAS BEEN LACKING

Direct federal involvement in highway public-private partnerships has generally been limited to projects in which federal requirements must be followed because federal funds have or will be used. At the time of our February 2008 report, minimal federal funding has been used in highway public-private partnerships. While direct federal involvement has been limited, the administration and the DOT have actively promoted highway public-private partnerships through policies and practices, including the development of experimental programs that waive certain federal regulations and encourage private investment. For example, until August 2007, federal regulations did not allow private contractors to be involved in highway contracts with a state department of transportation until after the federally mandated environmental review process had been completed. Texas applied for a waiver to allow its private contractor to start drafting a comprehensive development plan to guide decisions about the future of the corridor before its federal environmental review was complete. These flexibilities were pivotal to allowing highway public-private partnership arrangements in both Texas and Oregon to go forward while remaining eligible for federal funds. The Federal Highway Administration (FHWA) and DOT also promoted highway public-private partnerships by developing publications to educate state transportation officials about highway public-private partnerships and to promote their use, drafting model legislation for states to consider to enable highway public-private partnerships in their states, creating a public-private partnership Internet Web site, and making tolling a key component of DOT's congestion mitigation initiatives.

Recent highway public-private partnerships have involved sizable investments of funds and significant facilities and could pose national public interest implications such as interstate commerce that may transcend whether there is direct federal investment in a project. For example, both the Chicago Skyway and the Indiana Toll Road are part of the Interstate Highway System; the Indiana Toll Road is part of the most direct highway route between Chicago and New York City and, according to one study, over 60 percent of its traffic is interstate in nature. However, federal officials had little involvement in reviewing the terms of either of these concession agreements before they were signed. In the case of Indiana, FHWA played no role in reviewing either the lease or national public interests associated with leasing the highway, nor did it require the state of Indiana to review these interests. Texas envisions constructing new international border crossings and freight corridors using highway public-private partnerships, which may greatly facilitate North American Free Trade Agreement-related truck traffic to other states. However, no federal funding had been expended in the development of the project. Given the minimal federal funding in highway public-private partnerships to date, few mechanisms exist to consider potential national public interests in them. For example, FHWA officials told us that no federal definition of public interest or federal guidance on identifying and evaluating public interest exists.

The absence of a clear identification and furtherance of national public interests in the national transportation system is not unique to highway public-private partnerships. We have called for a fundamental reexamination of the nations surface transportation policies, including creating well-defined goals based on identified areas of national interest, incorporating performance and accountability into funding decisions, and more clearly defining the role of the federal government as well as the roles of state and local governments, regional entities, and the private sector. Such a reexamination provides an opportunity to identify emerging national public interests (including tax considerations), the role of the highway public-private partnerships in supporting and furthering those national interests, and how best to identify and protect national public interests in future public-private partnerships.

CONCLUDING OBSERVATIONS

Highway public-private partnerships show promise as a viable alternative, where appropriate, to help meet growing and costly transportation demands. The public sector can acquire new infrastructure or extract value from existing infrastructure while potentially sharing with the private sector the risks associated with designing, constructing, operating, and maintaining public infrastructure. However, highway public-private partnerships are not a panacea for meeting all transportation system demands, nor are they without potentially substantial costs and risks to the public—both financial and nonfinancial—and trade-offs must be made.

Highway public-private partnerships are fairly new in the United States, and, although they are meant to serve the public interest, it is difficult to be confident that these interests are being protected when formal identification and consideration of public and national interests has been lacking, and where limited up-front analysis of public interest issues using established criteria has been conducted. Consideration of highway public-private partnerships could benefit from more consistent, rigorous, systematic, up-front analysis. Benefits are potential benefits—that is, they are not assured and can only be achieved by weighing them against potential costs and trade-offs through careful, comprehensive analysis to determine whether public-private partnerships are appropriate in specific circumstances and, if so, how best to implement them.

Despite the need for careful analysis, the approach at the federal level has not been fully balanced, as DOT has done much to promote the benefits, but comparatively little to either assist states and localities weigh potential costs and trade-offs, nor to assess how potentially important national interests might be protected in highway public-private partnerships. We have suggested that

Congress consider directing the Secretary of Transportation to develop and submit objective criteria for identifying national public interests in highway public-private partnerships, including any additional legal authority, guidance, or assessment tools that would be appropriately required. We are pleased to note that in a recent testimony before the House, the Secretary indicated a willingness to begin developing such criteria. This is no easy task, however. The recent report by the National Surface Transportation Policy and Revenue Study Commission illustrates the challenges of identifying national public interests as the Policy Commission's recommendations for future restrictions—including limiting allowable toll increases and requiring concessionaires to share revenues with the public sector—stood in sharp contrast to the dissenting views of three commissioners.[6] We believe any potential federal restrictions on highway public-private partnerships must be carefully crafted to avoid undermining the potential benefits that can be achieved. Reexamining the federal role in transportation provides an opportunity for DOT, we believe, to play a targeted role in ensuring that national interests are considered, as appropriate.

Mr. Chairman, this concludes my prepared statement. I would be pleased to respond to any questions that you or other Members of the Subcommittee might have.

REFERENCES

[1]   GAO, Highway Public-Private Partnerships: More Rigorous Up-front Analysis Could Better Secure Potential Benefits and Protect the Public Interest, GAO-08-44 (Washington, D.C.: Feb. 8, 2008).

[2]   GAO, Highways and Transit: Private Sector Sponsorship of and Investment in Major Projects Has Been Limited, GAO-04-419 (Washington, D.C.: Mar. 25, 2004).

[3]   Depreciation is the accounting process of allocating against revenue the cost expiration of tangible property, plant, and equipment. Under straight-line depreciation, an equal amount of depreciation expense is taken annually over the life of the asset. Under accelerated depreciation, a depreciation expense is taken that is higher than annual straight-line amount in the early years and lower in later years.

[4]   GAO-04-419.

[5]   According to DOT officials, these projects were financed through models different than the public-private partnerships that are were the focus of our February 2008 report.

[6]   Transportation for Tomorrow, National Surface Transportation Policy and Revenue Study Commission, Dec. 2007.

INDEX

D

E